COMMUNICATION STUDIES

COMMUNICATION STUDIES

Preparing students for CAPE

EDLIN D. ROCHFORD

MEd Reading, BA (History and Literatures in English), Diploma in Education, Certificate in Speech and Language Pathology (University of the West Indies)

iUniverse, Inc.
Bloomington

COMMUNICATION STUDIES
PREPARING STUDENTS FOR CAPE

iUniverse books may be ordered through booksellers or by contacting:

iUniverse
1663 Liberty Drive
Bloomington, IN 47403
www.iuniverse.com
1-800-Authors (1-800-288-4677)

ISBN: 978-1-4620-5396-4 (sc)
ISBN: 978-1-4620-5397-1 (ebk)

Printed in the United States of America

iUniverse rev. date: 09/16/2011

Contents

Testimonials

This book was a very helpful source for me in preparations for my Communication Studies exams. I was able to obtain useful tips for my oral exams as well as listening comprehension. The past paper examples enabled me to see how the questions were structured. The notes in the book also helped in making my studies easier, as I was better able to answer past paper questions after studying the notes in the book. I was able to obtain a grade 1 in my exams and I am very happy that I purchased this book! I would, without hesitation recommend this book to all Communication Studies students!

Shinel Dore
6th Form Student, Nevis 6th Form College, Charlestown, Nevis

I have found this book to be extremely helpful during preparation for my CAPE Communication Studies exam. It is clear, concise and well-written, as well as handy in size. It comprehensively and systematically addresses each objective in the Communication Studies syllabus, while supplying readers with numerous examples to illustrate concepts which allow for better understanding. This book provided me with the essential material I needed for effective communication and for obtaining a high grade in my CAPE exam. I would highly recommend this book to anyone attempting this subject.

Simone Renwick
6th Form Student, Bishop Anstey High, Port of Spain

This book was very well-organized with straightforward explanations and very good examples so it was convenient to use as a quick reference on any topic. The small size also made it easy to carry around and helped me to make the most use of my time whether I was in the car or

just felt like laying down to read. It was of tremendous benefit to me in doing research and projects for my other subjects and then presenting that information in the best possible way.
Gabrielle Taylor
6th Form Student, Providence Girls High School, Port of Spain

Preface

My twenty-eight years of teaching covered pre-school, primary and secondary school. The range and diversity of students prepared me to rise to that great challenge to teach Communication Studies for the Caribbean Advanced Proficiency Examination (CAPE).

It was a relatively new subject in the Caribbean and thus there were no available texts. This eventually led me to cull my experience in writing this book, *Communication Studies: Preparing CAPE Students.* My double major in Literatures in English and History, coupled with my Post Graduate Diploma in Education proved of inestimable value in producing this seminal work. A special note of gratitude goes out to all the students who helped to hone my teaching skills during my career as they have all helped in paving the way for me to accomplish this work.

The following persons have all been either persuasive or supportive during the writing of *Communication Studies: Preparing CAPE Students.* My thanks to all of you and to those whom I may have forgotten to mention here.

My beloved Philip G Rochford HBM, my husband and coach who encouraged, supported and held me accountable!

The love and support of my family were crucial in the effort to complete this work. Special debt of gratitude to my brother in law Olav and sister, Alietha Vorren (Norway) for the unstinting support they gave in editing the manuscript.

Students of Bishop Anstey High School P-O-S, especially Sixth Form classes from 2007 to 2011 that had a 100% pass rate, thanks ladies for giving me the opportunity of possibility.

Special thanks to Ms Jade Murray who so readily gave me permission to use her portfolio as the sample. Thanks Jade!

This revision of the 2008 edition is in response to CAPE's modified syllabus of 2011.

OVERVIEW

i. Background and introduction

The ability to communicate is ranked first among the personal qualities of tertiary graduates sought by employers. Work experience was second, motivation third, academic credentials sixth and ethics tenth.
Report of the National Association of Colleges and Employers. (December 29, 1998). Wall Street Journal. Work Week, p. A1.

ii. Rationale for the CAPE Communication Studies

CAPE Communication Studies is a necessary subject given its aims and objectives.
The syllabus is focussed in such a way that it "integrates, enhances, deepens and broadens language skills and awareness already developed in the CSEC English A curriculum. It focuses *primarily* on the development of advanced competencies in *Standard English, particularly Caribbean Standard English.*[1] *At the same time; it attempts* to develop an appreciation of the linguistic diversity of the Caribbean . . ." CAPE Communication Studies Syllabus 2010.

iii. Competence in oral communication

Competence in oral communication—in speaking and listening—is prerequisite to your academic, personal, and professional success in life. Indeed, teachers deliver most instruction for classroom procedures orally to students. Students with ineffective listening skills fail to absorb much of the material to which they are exposed. Their problems are intensified when they respond incorrectly or inappropriately because of poor speaking skills. Students who cannot clearly articulate what they know may be wrongly judged as uneducated or poorly informed. Additionally, some speech styles of students can trigger stereotyped expectations of poor ability: expectations that may become self-fulfilling. Of equal concern, students who are unable to effectively ask for help from a teacher may not receive it, and typically reticent students progress more slowly despite what may be a normal level of aptitude.

iv. Oral communication for social adjustment

Beyond the confines of school, oral communication competence can contribute to individuals' social adjustment and participation in satisfying interpersonal relationships. Youngsters with poor communication skills are sometimes viewed as less attractive by their peers and enjoy fewer friendships. Antisocial and violent behavior often accompanies or occurs with underdeveloped social and conflict management skills. On the positive side, the ability to communicate orally supports sound psychological development. One's self concept is acquired through interaction with others. In psychological terms, achieving self-actualization involves communication activities such as making contributions in groups, exerting influence over others, and using socially acceptable behavior.

v. Oral communication in the work force

As individuals mature and become working adults, communication competence continues to be essential. Communication skills are required in most occupations. Employers identify communication as one of the basic competencies every graduate should have, asserting that the ability to communicate is valuable for obtaining employment and maintaining successful job performance. The communication skills essential in the workplace include basic oral and writing skills, and the ability to communicate in work groups or teams with persons of diverse background. Given the importance of the ability to communicate competently, then Communication Studies should be viewed as central in every secondary school. Humans are born with the ability to vocalize, but not with the knowledge, attitudes, and skills that define communication competence. *The ability to communicate effectively and appropriately is learned and therefore must be taught.*

Communication Studies: Preparing CAPE students seeks to provide credence for this argument as it covers the stipulated CAPE Communication Studies syllabus with the main aim to teach students to be effective communicators.

vi. Communication

The Merriam-Webster Online Dictionary defines ***communication*** as *"the exchange of thoughts, messages, of information, as by speech, signals, writing or behavior. The art and technique of using words effectively and with grace in imparting one's ideas."*

Communication can also be seen as the exchange of ideas, feelings or attitudes between two or more persons. You communicate continuously in many complex ways as you speak, scowl, write, preach, touch, smile, sit, stand, draw, cry or stare. All of these behaviors communicate an idea. Whether you communicate the intended message or not depends on your effective use of communication skills

Studies show that you communicate **55%** through your body language, **38%** through your tone of voice and **7%** verbally through your words. Communication Studies in the Sixth Form is not geared merely to introduce you to the subject but rather it is geared to develop you as whole persons, to improve the work of education, to advance the interests of society, to bridge cultural differences, and to advance you on the paths of your chosen careers.

MODULE 1: GATHERING and PROCESSING INFORMATION

At the end of Module 1 you are expected to be able to:

•	Speak and write with an acceptable control of grammar, vocabulary, mechanics, and conventions of Caribbean Standard English usage
•	Be able to identify the format and organizational features of the different genres and types of writing and speech
•	Evaluate the appropriateness of data collection methods
•	Apply any of *the different levels* of comprehension to examples of spoken and written material
•	Evaluate the effect of source, content, medium and channel on the reliability and validity of the information gathered
•	Gather, evaluate and present information about current issues *in an appropriately structured oral and written form*
•	Create a portfolio containing both oral and written work

1. Oral and Written forms of expression

The information learned in Module 1 is examined in Paper 1A (structured or short answers) and also in Paper 2 where you are required to answer in an essay format. In both your oral and written expression you are required to pay particular attention to grammar, usage, word choice, spelling, punctuation, pronunciation and enunciation. These are important elements in this subject as you are called upon to communicate both in the oral and written form.

2. Comprehension

Because reading is a thoughtful process, it embraces the idea of levels of comprehension."—Vacca & Vacca, 2005.

The term "levels of comprehension" refers to the thinking processes that are stimulated in order to arrive at answers to reading comprehension questions.

Literal comprehension refers to an understanding of the straightforward meaning of the text, such as facts, vocabulary, dates, times, and locations. Questions of literal comprehension can be answered directly and explicitly from the text. In our experiences working with teachers, we have found that they often check on literal comprehension first to make sure that their students have understood the basic or surface meaning of the text.

Literal comprehension questions are often asking you for details the writer has provided as support for or development of the main idea or central point.

With literal comprehension questions you can find the answers clearly stated in the passage, although the ideas may be paraphrased in the answer choices

Some literal comprehension questions start with phrases like these:

The passage states . . .

The writer states . . .

According to the passage . . .

According to the author . . .

Evaluation

Evaluation requires the learner to give a global or comprehensive judgment about some aspect of the text. For example, a comprehension question that requires the reader to give an evaluation of this article is: *How will the information in this article be useful to you?* In order to answer this type of question, students must use both a literal understanding of the text and their knowledge of the text's topic and related issues. Some students, because of cultural factors, may be reluctant to be critical or to disagree with the printed word.

3. Research

In this module as the main heading suggests, you are required to use as many skills as possible to gather and process information as you embark upon research. You are exposed to all the necessary tools needed to enable you to choose a portfolio topic and to complete this required portfolio sensibly. Appropriate use of language will be explored through examples of both the written and spoken forms of communication.

4. Why a focus on research and data collection skills?

The Communication Studies syllabus is designed to give you a wide range of skills, two of which are research and data collection. These skills are utilized when you begin to compile your portfolio on a teacher approved topic.

5. Starting your research

- The first step to research is to determine what it is that you wish to investigate
- The second step is to gather information through investigation
- The third step in the research process is to pull data from this information
- Data is specific and leads to the answers sought in research

6. Research is:

- A systematic process of collecting or gathering and analyzing data and information
- A systematic and organized way to find answers to questions.

- A process by which we find answers to questions.
- Investigation to gain information
- General information

7. **Research is not:**

- Mere information gathering
- Transportation of information/data/facts from one location to another
- Merely searching for information

8. **The characteristics of research**

- Research always originates with a question or a problem or hypothesis.
- Research always requires a clear articulation of a goal.
- Research always follows a specific plan of procedure.
- Research usually divides the principal problem into more manageable sub-problems.
- Research is always guided by the specific research problem, question, or hypothesis.
- Research accepts certain critical assumptions. These assumptions are underlying theories or ideas about how the world works.
- Research always requires the collection and interpretation of data in attempting to resolve the problem that initiated the research.

9. **The research process**

- Choosing the topic and asking the questions
- Identifying and locating sources
- Planning your search
- Hunting and gathering
- Sorting and organizing
- Making it your own

- Writing your findings
- Reviewing and Reflecting

Data and information

The terms ***data, information and knowledge*** are often used loosely and as though they are interchangeable.

Data can refer to facts, figures, numbers, text images or words, sounds that are obtained from experiments, observations or a set of premises. Data is used as the basis for making calculations or drawing conclusions. Data can be considered as the primary source of information.

Information **(i)** is knowledge which is definite, acquired or supplied about something or somebody.

Information **(ii)** is also gathered facts: the collected facts and data about a specific subject.

Information **(iii)** is the result of processing, gathering, manipulating and or organizing data in a way that adds to the knowledge of the receiver. In the broadest sense, information is anything that you are capable of perceiving.

Information **(iv)** can include written communications, spoken communications (verbal communication) photographs, art and music. Information may also be defined as data that has been meaningfully organized.

Traditionally, information in libraries was contained in books, periodicals, newspapers and other types of recorded media.

Data are mere facts that are independent in nature and unlimited in number. Information is the result of arranging data into meaningful knowledge. For example, a vehicle record may contain a number of data items such as the name of the vehicle, its model, cost, year of purchase, gasoline consumption, cost of repairs and maintenance, whether it was in an accident or even its colour. These data items can be linked to obtain useful information such as cost per mile of operation of a specific vehicle over a specific period of time. Consequently, information is always made up of data, but not all data may produce meaningful information.

Choosing your topic

In Module One you are expected to choose a *subject* for your Portfolio. Once you have chosen this subject, you must then narrow it into a *topic* by finding smaller aspects of the *subject*. This topic will then be the basis of your research paper.

A ***subject*** of a research paper is *the general and broad content and a* ***topic*** *is the specific issue being discussed.* You must be comfortable with the topic that you have chosen. Examples of some broad *subjects* are:

- **Foreign Foods in my country**
- **Local Foods v Foreign Foods**
- **Illegal Racing on our Roads**
- **Negative impact of Television**
- **The Elderly amongst us**
- **The Generation Gap**
- **Psychological Effects of Acne on Teenagers**
- **Fashion: Its importance to Youth**
- **West Indies Cricket**
- **The Importance of Goal Setting**
- **Extra curricular activities: Are they beneficial or not?**
- **Sibling Rivalry**
- **Cyber-Bullying**
- **The Pygmalion Effect on students**
- **The Middle Child Syndrome: Myth or Reality?**
- **Social Networks: Benefits or Addiction?**
- **Home-work: Benefit or Bother?**
- **Changes to the Family**
- **Fetishes that people have**
- **Teenage years: The Challenge**
- **Homelessness in my Country**
- **Coping with a Parent in Prison**
- **Living with a sick parent**
- **Living with an Illness**
- **Career choices**

- **Living with Unemployed Parents**
- **Local Tertiary Education v Foreign**
- **The Importance of Culture**
- **Fairy Tales v Folk Tales**
- **The Gender Divide**
- **The Issue of Discrimination (race/ethnicity, color, status, environment)**
- **Friendship: Give and Take or Take alone?**
- **Teenagers Obsession with Vampire Movies**
- **Addiction**

The *topic* of a Portfolio, in contrast, *is the specific issue being discussed.* Here are some possible topics for a Portfolio developed from the previous subjects:

- **Foreign Foods**
  Their impact on our health
- **Illegal Racing on our roads**
  What cause teenagers to race illegally?
  What measures can be put in place to deter this practice?
- **The Elderly amongst us**
  How are they seen and treated?
  How can they still be of service?
- **The Generation Gap**
  Is there a generation gap?
  What are the factors that caused this gap?
- **West Indies Cricket**
  Can they regain the glory years?
  What are the factors that caused the decline of West Indies cricket?
- **Psychological Effects of Acne on Teenagers**
  Effects on the family
  Alcohol's link to hard drugs
- **The Importance of Goal Setting**
  Where and when should it be taught?

Consider your subject from all angles as you strive to develop topics. You may wish to speak to other people, especially your teacher and persons who are trained and experienced in the subject matter. To get past the challenge of narrowing your topic to appropriate size, you can also try phrasing the subject as a question. Consult catalogs, reference books and textbooks for ideas.

Asking the questions

In this step, you need to define as clearly as possible the question that you want answered. After doing some simple background work on the topic then you may begin to formulate questions that will guide you along your way.

Identifying and locating sources

When you've chosen your topic and have formulated the questions that you will ask, then you need to know where to locate these materials. Sources are available in both print and electronic formats. The internet is a great medium for sourcing both Primary and Secondary sources. On the internet you can find electronics sources such as Online Library Collections and Online Databases. The printed sources which you can choose from include such materials as catalogues, journals, newspapers and books on the specific topic. See the section in this Module on ***Reliability of Internet Sources.***

Planning your search

Because the list of available sources can be inexhaustible, you need to prioritize your questions and your action/ search time.

Gathering information

Gather all the information that you feel you will need.

Sorting and organizing your information

Use the methods of skimming and scanning to help you identify what you really need for your research.

Making it your own

Once you have gathered all the information that you need, you make it your own by adding your own interpretation of it. You do this by way of analysis, logical comparison, and argument.

Writing your findings

Who is your audience? What is the tone and style of communication that you are using? Who and what are your sources? What will your bibliography look like? What medium or channel you are using to present your findings?
Generally presentations can take the forms of PowerPoint presentation, a research paper, a video, compact disc and DVD. However, for purposes of the CAPE Communication Studies, all presentations take the forms of the seven to nine minute oral presentation to your teacher and the final written compilation of your Portfolio. See the section in this Module on ***Portfolio Preparation*** for further information.

Reviewing and reflecting

In this step, you are looking back at the process that you have used, reflecting on how it can be enhanced and doing a general evaluation. When searching for information on a topic, it is important to understand the value of both primary and secondary sources.

*A **primary source in this context** is an original document containing firsthand information about a topic. Primary sources are therefore documents or other sources of information that are created at or near the time/situation being researched.* Persons themselves often document primary sources.

Different fields of study may use different types of primary sources. Some common examples of a primary source are:

- Diaries
- Interviews
- Letters
- Original works of art
- Photographs
- Memoirs
- Autobiographies
- Works of literature

A ***secondary source*** *contains commentary on or discussion about a primary source.* The most important feature of secondary sources is that they offer an *interpretation* of information gathered from primary sources. Some common examples of a secondary source are:

- Biographies
- Dissertations
- Indexes, Abstracts, Bibliographies (used to locate a secondary source)
- Films and documentaries
- Journal Articles
- Monographs

10. Primary and secondary sources

Primary sources are first hand sources and ***secondary sources*** are second-hand sources. For example, let us suppose there had been a car accident. The description of the accident which a witness gives to the police is a primary source because it comes from someone actually there at the time and would have witnessed the accident. The story in the newspaper the next day is a secondary source because the reporter who wrote the story did not actually witness it. The reporter is presenting a way of understanding the accident or an interpretation of the eyewitness account.

However, the distinctions between primary and secondary sources can be a bit blurred. An individual document may be a primary source in one context and a secondary source in another. Time is a defining element. For example, a recent newspaper article is not usually a primary source; but a newspaper article from the 1960's may be a primary source for information on many of the region's journey towards independence.

Table of primary sources			
Annual Reports	Eye-witness accounts	Memos	Photographs
Autobiographies		Membership lists	Raw data
Census reports	Court hearings	Immigration papers	Sources/ Informants
Correspondences	Interviews	Newspaper articles	Speeches
Court cases	Letters	Original works of art/literature	Statutes
Diary/journal	Birth/death/ marriage records	Personal writings/ narratives	Tax reports
e-mails	Meeting minutes	Personal accounts	Minutes
Blog entries	Memoirs	Newsletters	

Table of secondary sources	
Almanacs	Dissertation
Bibliographies	Encyclopedias
Biographies	History books
Books	Journal/Magazine/Newspaper articles
Commentaries	Reference books
Critical studies/Criticism	Textbooks

11. Acknowledging your sources

It is very important to acknowledge your sources so as to give credit to the person or persons from whose information you use and also so as allow others the privilege of checking to verify or clarify the source.

12. Checklist for choosing your topic

So is this your final topic? Are you truly satisfied? Try this checklist.

- ***Is my topic still too broad?*** Check your sources. How many pages do they devote to the topic? If it takes other writers a book to answer the question you have decided on, then your topic is still too big!
- ***Is my topic too limited?*** Is the topic perfect for a 300-to-500 word essay? If so it is too narrow for your Expository section of your portfolio where it belongs. Typically a student needs to present orally for 7 to 9 minutes and as such the expected word limit should be 700 to 800 words.
- ***Is my topic tedious?*** Been there, done that! If your topic bores you before you have even started writing, you can bet it will bore your audience. Your audience in this case is made up of your teacher and your classmates to whom you might present.
- ***Is my topic too controversial?*** If you are afraid of offending your audience with your topic, do not take the risk. Choose a topic with which both you and your audience are comfortable.

13. Effective Listening

An important aspect of communication is ***listening***. Effective listening is hearing and understanding the message being sent, and using body language to confirm that you are listening. The greatest tribute that one human being can pay to another human being is to listen to that person as he or she speaks. Within any communication there are two key elements: the person communicating and the person receiving the message. The communicator at times becomes the listener and the listener at times becomes the communicator. To be an effective person in your environment you must master the art of listening and communicating in order to complete the communication loop.

In Communication Studies you are expected to accomplish effective listening when you are called upon to undertake a listening comprehension exercise. In this exercise you are given the questions about a passage beforehand and then the teacher reads the passage, during which you are allowed to take copious notes based on the questions. Sometimes because you may have not been trained to listen effectively you become distracted during the exercise and valuable information is lost. The trick in listening comprehension is to be able to listen and distinguish what information you need as against what you do not need based on the questions that you are given.

14. Improving your listening skills

- *Always have an open mind about the person speaking.*
  Your mind and a parachute have this in common. They are only useful when open.
- *Listen from the first sentence.*
  The first few sentences often contain clues to understanding the whole conversation. Therefore you must listen from the first word.
- *Concentrate on what is being said.*
  If your attention is other than on what is being said, miscommunication and misunderstanding will occur.
- *Conquer the temptation to interrupt.*
  Practice this rule now. The next person you speak to, resolve not to interrupt when that person is speaking. It will be a revelation to you.

- *Clarify meaning and stimulate others to talk by asking questions.*
  Look for what is important, but not being said.
- *Note important points as the conversation progresses.*
- *Be conscious of your facial expressions and body language.*
  They show what you are thinking.
- *Avoid reacting to highly emotive words.*

15. Tips for your listening comprehension exercise

The average student spends about 25 hours per week in class listening or perhaps I should say "hearing" (there is a difference) to lectures. You can improve your listening skills by following some of the strategies below:

(1) ***Maintain eye contact with the teacher.*** Of course you will need to look at your paper to write your notes, but eye contact keeps you focused on the job at hand and keeps you involved in the reading exercise.

(2) ***Focus on content, not delivery.*** Have you ever counted the number of times a teacher clears his/her throat in a fifteen minute period? If so, you weren't focusing on content. In this listening comprehension exercise you are given the list of questions prior to the teacher's reading of the passage. Focus on making the right notes to help you answer the questions.

(3) ***Avoid emotional involvement.*** When you are too emotionally involved in listening, you tend to hear what you want to hear and not what is actually being said. Try to remain objective and open-minded.

(4) ***Avoid distractions.*** Don't let your mind wander or be distracted by the person shuffling papers near you. If the classroom is too hot or if it's raining outside or if you are tempted to stare out the window

try, to remedy that situation if you can. The solution may require that you sit near a fan or sit away from the window.

(5) ***Treat listening as a challenging mental task.*** Listening in your classroom to a teacher is not a passive act or at least it shouldn't be. You need to concentrate on what is said so that you can process the information into your notes and eventually into the correct answers.

(6) ***Remain active by asking mental questions.*** Active listening keeps you on your toes. Here are some questions you can ask yourself as you listen. What key point is the teacher making? How does this fit with the questions on the paper in front of me?

16. Factors which affect effective listening

- Distractions of any kind: for example, if you are ill, if you are worried or if you are tired you cannot listen effectively
- Environmental noises: for example, if there is a construction site nearby or if the room is unsuitable
- If you have problems with your hearing ability
- If the speaker is unprepared or if her mode of delivery is poor.

17. Different ways of reading

You *skim* to get an overview or the general gist of the material. You *scan* when you know what you are looking for and you are reading to find that particular piece of information in the material. When you scan, the material is fully covered. You do *critical reading* when you want to identify the writer's intent, purpose and language techniques and strategies used.

18. Organizational features of written and oral works

- Topic or thesis sentence or introduction

- Content or body
- Logical linkages or transitional words
- Formatting
- Conclusion or summary
- Revising and editing drafts

19. Data collection

Data collection source is the mechanism or method for collecting data such as surveys, focus group discussions, observations and interviews.

Data collection instrument is the physical tool used to collect the data such as checklists, clients or students' record cards, class registers and questionnaires.

20. Readily available data

- Files or records
- Computer databases
- Government reports
- Other reports or prior evaluations
- Census data or statistical data
- Documents such as budgets, policies and procedures and maps

You can also get information from ***expert judgment*** where the experts are persons with areas of expertise, diverse perspectives and political viewpoints.

21. Choosing the right data collection methods

Once you have started a portfolio with a particular collection method it is very hard to change and that is why it is very important to make the right selection from the beginning. Your choice of method should be a pragmatic decision that is based on the needs of the project.

22. Data collection methods

Methods are the instruments/tools that you use to investigate and to discover *what you need to know* in order to help you in your research. Methods are often divided into two categories: qualitative and quantitative approaches.

The word *qualitative* implies an emphasis on processes and meanings that are not rigorously examined or measured (if measured at all), in terms of quantity, amount, intensity, or frequency. Qualitative researchers stress the socially constructed nature of reality, the intimate relationship between the researcher and what is studied, and the situational constraints that shape inquiry. In contrast, *quantitative* studies emphasize the measurement and analysis of causal relationships between variables not processes.

23. Categories of methods

- ***Interviews***—Different types of interviews provide different types of data. For example, an *in-depth, informal* interview can produce qualitative information, whereas a highly *structured* and *scripted* interview can produce more quantitative results. Some interviews can be structured like a questionnaire or an informal discussion, or conducted with individuals or groups. Interviews can be done in one session or they can be arranged as a series of interviews.
- ***Questionnaires***—They are a very popular method of research, but can vary a great deal on how they are implemented, for example questionnaires can be sent out by post, face to face, by telephone or even via the internet. All of these factors can influence the outcomes of interviews and therefore the usefulness of the exercise.

- ***Observation***—This can happen on a range of observer and participant relationships. However, issues of confidentiality and ethical behavior can be problematic.
- ***Journals***—Observer and participant diaries or journals can produce interesting qualitative information over a given period of time.
- ***Case studies***—Detailed information about a particular subject or small group. The qualitative information received allows for conclusions to be drawn only about that subject or small group and only in that specific context.
- ***Secondary sources of data***—This can be very helpful in the earliest stage of a research project when the right questions are still being defined. For example, *previous research reports* can form the basis of a new and updated research project.
- ***Experiments***—These are not used often in social scientific research as they are based on natural scientific methods. However, they are useful when specific controls are added to the planning process and detailed outcomes are defined. For example, examining the responses of two diverse groups undertaking similar examinations and comparing the results according to ethnicity and gender of the participants.

It is possible however, to combine and mix different research methods for different parts of your project.

24. Types of research study

Most research projects fit into one of three ideal typologies:

Evaluation—These research studies examine the effects of a strategy that has been implemented.

Strategy and changes—This type of study investigates and informs developmental issues. By analyzing a particular problem area, research findings can advise and lead to changes in future policy or service provision.

Targets and trends—The analysis of certain targets and trends is very common typology employed to broadly investigate patterns of results.

25. Factors to consider when choosing your research method

As well as choosing the ideal methods of research for a project we also need to consider other factors and criteria such as:

(1) ***Cost***—Undertaking a large scale questionnaire survey would be expensive to circulate by postage and to process the data collected would be labor intensive. Similarly, undertaking the observation method can be expensive as in many cases you would have to employ highly-trained researchers.

(2) ***Expertise***—Locating and employing particularly skilled researchers is crucial to achieving the goals of a research.

(3) ***Timescales***—The use of detailed interviews and large scale surveys can be time-consuming and overrun the research projects timescale. Although interviews can be relatively short, much time is needed to properly analyze all the collected data.

(4) ***Reliability***—All research methods need the capacity to estimate how easy it is the make general findings applicable to wider contexts. For example, does the instrument consistently give the same results with the same group of people under the same conditions? Reliability has within it a level of accuracy, dependability and stability.

(5) ***Validity***—All research methods must allow the researcher and audience to evaluate the validity of what was intended to be measured.

(6) ***Ethics***—Ensure that your research method permits that participants have the freedom to refuse to take part in the study, without the integrity of your research design being compromised. The best methodology in theory and on paper may not work when people are involved. A Code of Practice should be employed.

(7) ***Accessibility***—Remember that however good the design methodology appears on paper, it will be useless if the

intended subjects and participants cannot be accessed by the process. For example, if you chose questionnaires as your method but because of various reasons were not able to distribute the intended amount, then the problem was with accessibility.

26. **How much information should you collect?**

Sampling refers to selecting a portion of a population in order to learn something about the entire population without having to measure the whole group. In other words sampling is a representative portion of the whole.

There are two types of sampling methods: *random* and *purposive*. ***Random*** methods are used to produce samples that are to a certain extent free from bias. In a random sampling each person in the population has an equal choice of being chosen for the sample.

Purposive methods are used to produce a sample that will represent specific viewpoints of particular groups. The purposive sample consists of individuals who are handpicked or selected deliberately by the researcher.

27. **The strengths and weaknesses of research methods**

Direct/Participant Observations are methods by which a person or persons are able to gather first hand data on the subject being studied.

Strengths of Observations

- Able to gather objective data
- Addition of observer's insights
- Provide direct information about behavior of individuals and groups
- Exist mostly in natural, unstructured and flexible environment
- Can develop a holistic perspective

Weaknesses of Observations

- Potential to misinterpret observation
- Time consuming
- Difficult to carry out because persons may become suspicious of an observer
- The observers' presence may cause bias
- Expensive
- Display of atypical behavior from subjects being studied

Focus Groups

These groups have a combination of elements from both interviews and participant observations. They are generally a gathering of 8 to 12 persons who came together to discuss a selected topic of interest that is relevant to the research that is being undertaken. These are useful in the initial stage of the research.

Strengths of Focus Groups

- More accurate information because respondents are less likely to give inaccurate answers knowing that they may be contradicted by other members.
- Group synergy enables members to share without being intimidated
- Low cost and quick to initiate
- Greater pool of expertise is tapped.

Weaknesses of Focus Groups

- Data is difficult to analyze
- Need careful training
- Groups vary and can be difficult to assemble
- One or more participants may dominate the views

Interviews

Provide very different data from observations as they allow the interviewer to capture different perspectives. Interviews are selected when interpersonal contact is important. There are two types of interviews used in research: *structured interviews,* in which a carefully constructed questionnaire is administered and *in-depth interviews* which are more flexible and encourage free and open responses.

Strengths of Interviews

- Greater depth of information that is rich in data, details and new insights
- Allows extensive probing and open-ended questions
- Permits face to face contacts with respondents
- Allows interviewer to explain and clarify questions thus eliciting useful responses

Weaknesses of Interviews

- Subjectivity
- Require train interviewers
- Expensive and time-consuming
- Interviewer may distort information because of selective perception
- Volume of information too large resulting in difficulty in transcribing

Surveys

- Are done when there is a need to collect information that is not available from other sources.
- Allow the person conducting them to obtain the attitudes, opinions, and behaviors of the sampling.
- Allow one to compare information and then make meaningful analysis

Surveys can be conducted

- Written
- Via the mail or postal service
- On-line via the e-mail or internet
- In person or face to face
- Via the telephone

> ***A note about questionnaires***
>
> **Very importantly the questions** on a questionnaire should be designed with the intended respondents in mind. Thus, it should take into consideration their educational background and personal experience.

Questionnaires must

- Contain questions that the respondents are familiar with
- Contain simple language
- Avoid painful or embarrassing questions
- Not ask for more than one piece of information at a time
- Avoid ambiguous worded questions
- Start with easier questions
- Ask all the respondents the questions in exactly the same way

In deciding which methods you will like to use you may wish to consider the following

- What do you want to know?
- What assessment topics do you want to cover and what indicators do you want to use?
- Who would provide this information; persons such as your neighborhood residents, experts, other students or teachers?
- What resources do you have such as time, money, volunteers or readily available data?

- What is your deadline for having this information?

Once you have answered these questions, look at the following ***summary chart*** to determine which data collection methods are right for you. The methods you choose depend on your answers to the above questions. Generally, the more methods you choose, the better results you get, but the more resources you would need.

28. Summary chart of data collection methods

Methods	Advantages	Disadvantages
Interviews	Provide detailed responses. Provide clear context to questions. Use smaller samples groups. Provide subjects' point of view.	Opportunity for interviewer bias to intervene. Can be time consuming. Can be difficult to analyze. The findings reliability and validity can be affected as statistical inference cannot be provided.
Questionnaires	Involve large target audience and allow statistical analysis. Anonymous, easy to organize and cost effective. Validity and reliability can be measured. Trends can be identified by asking the same questions over time.	Some answers can be incomplete. Respondent may misinterpret questions. Low response rates may be received. Information collected may be limited by pre-determined answer choices and question categories.

Ethnography	Demonstrates the meaning of events in the context of a lifetime. Diminishes chance of researchers pre-selecting data by the questions they ask.	Hard to build general observations from individual study. Data analysis and ethical problems can occur.
Observation	Complete and non-intrusive. Produces detailed understanding of situation/processes. Very useful for studying behavioral processes.	Can be time consuming and analysis can be complicated. Difficult to gain access to subjects. Data maybe specific to the observed setting and non-transferable. Large amounts of data are produced. Observer bias
Secondary sources	Inexpensive and allow access to large data sets. Reduced data collection. Bigger picture provided from data from different sources.	Difficult to compare data from different sources. No control over research design of information. Data collected may not be reliable to start with.
Case studies	They provide the opportunity for detailed research analysis. They provide a clear context for research and examples of good/bad practice.	Similar problems as with interviews can occur. Anecdotal data can be produced, with a poor evidence context.

Focus Groups	Group discussion Participants can build on each other's comments Can be quicker than a survey Can be less costly Can reach more people than interviews Can hear a variety of ideas and opinions Participants can take advantage of the shared experience	A group or an individual can dominate the session. Some opinions may not be heard in a group discussion. Success depends on group participation in discussion. Information gathered may not represent the larger community. Smaller numbers reached
Surveys	Can reach large numbers of people. Questions can focus responses as either very specific or open-ended Can establish relationships among indicators.	No in-depth responses on issues. Does not allow respondents to exchange ideas Limited to specific questions. May not reach people who are hard to reach Telephone & written surveys have poor returns.

29. Portfolio preparation

At this point you should have selected your topic and/or specific theme for your portfolio. The topic must be one on which both primary and secondary information are readily available. *Your teacher has the final say.* Remember that your research is directed to answering a research question. Begin early to gather information on your topic so as not to be overwhelmed at the end. Organize your portfolio into smaller tasks and stay within the completion due date.

Your Portfolio is divided into three sections: Expository, Reflective and Analytical.

PORTFOLIO
Expository
Reflective
Analytical

30. Expository

In this section of the Portfolio you are required to make a seven to nine minute oral presentation to your teacher based on the topic of your choice. Most teachers utilized their option to have their students conduct a "mock oral presentation" in the classroom with their classmates as the audience. At least two pieces of pertinent or relevant information on the chosen topic must be collected. These articles may be utilized in your presentation and then placed in your overall portfolio. For example if you chose to compile a portfolio on the topic of ***"The Importance of Fashion to Teenagers"*** then two relevant pieces of information can be articles collected from newspapers or from the internet or an excerpt from a text. Students must pay particular attention to the fact that their oral presentation is not an essay and should contain specific factors.

In your presentation you should:

- Have a clear introduction.
- Have an explanation of the chosen topic and reason for the choice
- Discuss at least three or four issues pertaining to the topic. Issues may be put forward as questions that you or others have about the topic.
- Discuss the challenges that you experienced or encountered as you conducted your research

- Make an evaluation of the effectiveness of the source. For example were you able to corroborate the information that you got from the various sources? Or were there gaps in the information that you collected?
- Evaluate the effect of context and medium or channel on the reliability and validity of the information in their research
- Have a clear conclusion

See the section on *Improving your Presentation Skills* in Module Three. (page 111)

31. Identifying Issues in your topic

For purposes of your oral presentation an issue may be defined as a subject or problem which people are thinking and talking about, or most important of what is being discussed. Some students find it difficult to identify clear issues in their presentation and as such it turns out to be nothing more than an essay. The following are some pointers that will help you to identify the issues for your oral presentation:

- What is the critical problem? Explicitly state the problem. Are you sure it is a problem? Is it important? What would happen if the "problem" were left alone? Could attempts to solve the "problem" result in unintended consequences?
- Where is the problem? Is it an individual, relationships, group, intergroup, leadership/motivation/power, or a complete system?
- Why is it a problem? Is there a "gap"? What information is lacking? For whom is it a problem and why?
- Can the problem be solved permanently or will it occur again? Is this problem masking a deeper systemic problem?
- How do key people feel about the problem and current outcomes? If you had a chance to talk to or interview the critical players, what would you want to know? Who would most likely have the information you need?

- How urgent is the problem? How important is the problem relative to other problems?

Some Traps to Avoid

- Failing to consider the possibility of multiple causes.
- Confusing symptoms with causes—is there something else going on to make the problem appear or make it worse?
- Failing to differentiate fact from opinion.
- Prematurely suggesting a solution.
- Stating the problem as a disguised solution (e.g. "we need more . . .").

Remember that:

- You will often **not have all the information** you would like.
- There is **rarely one "right" answer**—more than one solution may be possible.
- One of most critical yet most difficult aspect of case analysis may be i**dentifying the problem**, BUT you may never be sure you have identified the real problem.
- Accept that most situations often involve:

    a. ambiguous situations
    b. multiple casualties
    c. inadequate information
    d. no one elegant solution

- Some problems **may have "no solution"**, but it's important to do the analysis.

32. **Reflective section**

- One sample of your original work. The sample should be no more than 800 words.

- A **Preface** of no more than 200 words must accompany your reflective piece.

33. Examples of genres

- A poem
- Diary entry or entries
- Journal entry or entries
- A play or skit
- A song on CD with accompanying lyrics
- A eulogy
- A monologue
- A short story
- Letter (s) to the Editor
- Argumentative Essay

Criteria for Marking the Reflective Piece

Students' original sample of work will be marked according to:

- **Creativity** in terms of what is unique to the specific genre that you have chosen and the originality of your ideas and the events of the story
- **Organizational factors** in terms of a well defined introduction, development of the issues in the content, all round coherence and cohesion.
- **Expression** in terms of appropriateness of register to the chosen genre, grammatical language, punctuation and careful proofreading.

34. General Introduction

- This section should be no more than **200 words.**
- You should relate specifically to the Expository, Reflective and Analytical sections stating what aspects of the theme or topic will be developed in each of these three sections.

- You should clearly identify the ***theme*** or the topic which you have selected.
- You should state the ***purpose*** of selecting your topic or theme. (Your purpose should not be "*I have chosen this topic because I have to do a topic for CAPE*")
- You should show how your topic relates to your ***academic interests***. For example can it help you with other content area subjects or even with school matters?
- You should show how your topic can be connected to your ***future career choice***. Some students at this point are unable to see any connection and as such do not write any, but it is advisable to be creative and state a connection.
- You should state your ***personal interest*** in this topic.
  See Exhibit "G" for a complete sample of the Portfolio.

Criteria for Marking the General Introduction

Many students make the mistake of not addressing sufficiently the section titled "**How theme is treated in the Exposition and Reflection sections.**" In this section you will be marked in terms of:

- Your explanation of how your theme is developed in the Exposition by giving which aspects of your theme will be developed here.
- Your explanation of how your theme is developed in the Reflection section by giving which aspects of your theme will be developed here.
- How each section contributes to achieving the purpose of this portfolio?

35. Preface

- Clearly state your *theme* of your portfolio.
- The *purpose* for writing this reflective piece. An example of a *purpose* can be that you hope that by doing this piece you

will be able to use it as a medium to create awareness or to sensitize teenagers about the potential dangers of illegal road—racing.

- Identify the *intended* or *target audience* and be specific in terms of age, gender, and background.
- The *context or situation* in which this selection can be used. For example the play that you have written for your reflective may be used in a school assembly that is focused on highlighting the dangers of illegal racing. It may be used especially as some students got injured when they were involved in racing illegally on our nation's roads. Context in the Preface refers to where or in what situation your reflective can be used effectively and not to any situation in your reflective.
- Some further contexts in which your pieces may be used can be: In a Website on the topic, in your own Blog, in a PowerPoint, in a CD, a DVD, in letters to the Editor, on a Facebook page and as an excerpt read on a Television or Radio program on the topic.

<u>This section should be no more than 200 words!</u>

Criteria for Marking the Preface

- You must provide ***specific*** evidence of your ***purpose*** for writing this piece.
- Be ***specific*** about your ***audience***. For example your topic in most case is audience specific and you should pay attention to this.
- Provide the ***specific context*** or contexts in which maximum benefits can be achieved from the use of this piece.

36. Analytical section

When making your choice of genre for your *Reflective* section, keep in mind that this original piece is to be used in your analytical section.

Remember that as the author of your original piece you must ensure that it contains all the four elements of registers, dialectal variation, attitudes to language and communicative behaviors, even though *only two of these will be analyzed.* Some students are creating their original piece with only the two elements that they chose to analyze but there are two weaknesses to this practice. Firstly your original piece will be lacking all the elements which make it complete and secondly you are allowing yourself no room for choice when there are only two elements in your piece. Your original piece should contain all of these elements:

- Registers
- Varied forms of dialects
- Differing attitudes to language displayed by the characters in the piece
- Communicative behaviors

<u>This analytical piece should be no longer than 350 words!</u>

Criteria for marking your analysis based on content, expression and organization

- You must provide evidence of analysis of your two chosen elements
- Your analysis must show clear and fluent control of grammar and syntax
- Your analysis must be organized showing clear introduction, development using linking or transitional words, coherence and conclusion.

37. Types of writings

There are basically four types or modes of discourse that writers may utilize individually or in a combination, to achieve the specific purpose they intended. These four types can be identified as description, exposition, narration and argument.

In a *descriptive* piece of writing the main function or purpose is to express to the reader what a thing looks like, feels like, tastes like, smells like or sounds like. In other words a descriptive discourse requires the readers to use one or more of their senses. In a descriptive piece we get sensuous details about persons, places, feelings, and times. One's sense of visualization is able to summon a visual image of whatever is described. If this does not happen during or after reading then the piece was not successful in its delivery.

In an *exposition* the purpose is to bring clarity to ideas, to analyze a situation, to define a given term, and to issue instruction. An expository piece gives the readers information whilst explaining the ideas. This is the most common type of discourse used by persons. Below is a list of devices used in exposition.

- Analysis
- Classification
- Definition
- Illustration
- Cause and effect
- Comparison and contrast
- Analogy

A *narrative* piece is concerned with actions and seeks to present to the readers a sense of what any person witnesses in any action. Many persons associate the word narrative with storytelling but, narratives cover any type of discourse that relate to events that occur in a specific period of time. Narratives include short stories, novels, historical stories and the giving of instructions on how to do something where a process is involved.

In an *argumentative* piece the emphasis is on persuading or convincing the reading audience that the writer's claims are true. There is much appeal to reason and/ or emotion. Argumentative pieces focus on beliefs, attitudes, ideas and conceptions.

TYPES OF WRITINGS
Descriptive
Expositive
Narrative
Argumentative

38. What is a genre?

Genre is a word from the French which means "category." Genre is "a *term used in literary criticism to designate the distinct types or categories into which literary works are grouped according to form or technique.*" (*Dictionary of Literary Terms*) Books that belong to the same genre have things in common. For example mystery books contain stories that are written around a puzzling situation that you the reader tries to figure out. Biography is another genre that tells the facts about someone's life and personality.

39. Different types of genres

Different genres—that is, different types of literature such as epics, lyrics, sonnet, elegies, comedies, tragedies, novels, short stories, vignettes, essays, non-fiction prose, and autobiographies—demand different ways of reading. When we read we try to identify the many literary techniques or devices specific to the genre of the work. More accurately, we read presupposing that we will encounter experiences to which we can relate and we base our discernment upon the devices employed in that genre.

Tone is the writer's or speaker's attitude toward the subject of the passage. Tone may be communicated through words and details that express particular emotions and that evoke an emotional response in the reader or listener.

40. Levels of comprehension

Reading is a thinking activity which involves the reader getting meaning from the printed word or symbol. As secondary students you are expected to be able to read at **all** levels of meaning or comprehension. Levels in this case refer to the different depths of understanding and different analysis of what is meant. In other words, you will be expected to read and maneuver your way through the **literal**, **interpretiv**e and **applied** level of comprehension.

Level One is the *Literal level* where the student responds with what were actually stated giving facts and details. At this level there is

- Rote learning and memorization
- Only surface learning taking place.
- Tests given in this category contain objectives that deal with true / false, multiple choice and fill-in-the blank questions.
- Common questions used to elicit this type of thinking are who, what, when, and where questions.

Level Two is the *Interpretive level* where the student responds by stating what was implied or meant rather than what was actually stated. At this level students also:

- Draw inferences
- Tap into prior knowledge / experience
- Attach new learning to old information
- Make logical leaps and educated guesses
- Read between the lines to determine what is meant by what is stated.

Tests given in this category are subjective, and the types of questions asked are open-ended, thought-provoking questions beginning with why, what if, and how.

Level Three is the *Applied level* where firstly the students' responses contain what was said on a *litera*l level. Secondly they respond by saying what was meant by what was said on the *interpretive* and then finally they extend the concepts or ideas beyond the situation. At this level students may also:

- Analyze
- Synthesize
- Apply

The charts below give you some extra concepts that you are expected to be able to manipulate at each level of comprehension.

Level 1: Information or knowledge

Cite	Identify	Name	Recognize	State
Count	Indicate	Point	Record	Tabulate
Define	Label	Quote	Relate	Tell
Describe	List	Read	Repeat	Trace
Draw	Locate	Recite	Select	Write

Level 2: Comprehension

Associate	Convert	Estimate	Illustrate	Report
Classify	Describe	Expand	Interpolate	Restate
Compare	Differentiate	Explain	Interpret	Review
Compute	Discuss	Express	Locate	Summarize
Contrast	Distinguish	Extrapolate	Predict	Translate

Level 3: Application

Apply	Demonstrate	Interpolate	Practice	Schedule
Calculate	Dramatize	Interpret	Predict	Sketch
Choose Procedures	Employ	Locate	Relate	Solve
Collect	Examine	Operate	Report	Translate
Information	Find	Order	Restate	Use
Complete	Solutions	Perform	Review	Utilize
Construct	Illustrate			

Level 4: Analysis

Analyze	Criticize	Diagram	Generalize	Organize
Appraise	Debate	Differentiate	Infer	Question
Conclude	Detect	Distinguish	Inspect	Separate
Contract	Determine	Experiment	Inventory	Summarize

Level 5: Synthesis

Arrange	Construct	Formulate	Manage	Prescribe
Assemble	Create	Generalize	Organize	Produce
Collect	Design	Integrate	Plan	Propose
Compile	Detect	Invent	Prepare	Specify
Compose	Develop			

Level 6: Evaluation

Appraise	Contrast	Develop	Measure	Revise
Assess	Criteria	Estimate	Rank	Score
Choose	Critique	Evaluate	Rate	Select
Compare	Decide	Grade	Recommend	Test
Conclude	Determine	Judge		

NB: Some of these concepts in the charts above may be useful for describing a writer's intention in Module 1 essay.

41. Addressing the requirements of Module One Essay

In Paper 02 the Module One essay asks you to *identify* the writer's ***main point*** or ***main idea***, the writer's ***purpose or intention*** and comment on organizational strategies and language techniques used to achieve the purpose. You are also required to make specific references to the passage to support the strategies and the techniques. It is important that you respond if not immediately then specifically to the differing parts of the question. Some students ramble on, skirting around the answer but sadly never directly answering the question. Write directly to each part of the question!

- The writer's main point or idea ***cannot be*** expressed as the purpose. Some students make the mistake of writing the main idea and the purpose in one sentence. For example it is incorrect to say "*In this extract the writer's main point and purpose is to discuss the immense destructive power of tsunamis and the disastrous effects they can have on areas.*" There is a ***distinction*** between the main point and the purpose and in this case no mark will be awarded to you.

- The writer's main point or main idea is what the passage is all about. Simply put the main point is the focus of the passage. There should not be a verb or action word in your statement of the main point. An example is: *The writer's main point or main idea is* ***that tsunamis are vast, speedy, high-energy bodies of far-travelling seawater that can create or wreak havoc to countries.***

- The writer's purpose or intention is what the writer hope to achieve by writing. In most cases the writer's purpose is always to bring the message of the main point to the readers or the audience. Unlike the main point where there no verb, the purpose contains a verb. Using the same main point, then the purpose will either be to "***sensitize, alert, educate, create awareness, create a sense of imminent or potential danger that tsunamis with their tremendous vast and speed can have on countries.***

- The use of words such as "*to show*", "*to inform*", "*to notify*" will only earn you the minimum of marks.

- Always connect the writer's main point with his or her purpose.

42. Writer's Purpose

When you communicate with others you are usually guided by some purpose, goal or aim. You may wish to **express y**our feelings. You may want simply to **explore** an idea or perhaps **entertain** or **amuse y**our listeners or readers. You may wish to **inform** people or **explain** an idea. You may wish to **argue** for or against an idea in order to **persuade** others to believe or act in a certain way. You make special kinds of arguments when you are **evaluating** or **problem solving.** Finally, you may wish to **mediate** or **negotiate** a solution in a tense or difficult situation.

Remember however, that very often writers **combine different purposes** in a single piece of writing. For example, in a report you may begin by informing readers of the economic facts before you try to persuade them to take a certain course of action.

A purpose is the *aim or goal* of the writer of the written product and a strategy is a *means* of achieving that purpose. For example, your purpose may be to explain something but you may use definitions, examples, descriptions, and analysis in order to make your explanation clearer. A variety of strategies are available for writers to help them find ways to achieve their purpose. A simple way of identifying what is the writer's purpose is to remember that a purpose is ***always to do something.***

43. How audience and focus affect your purpose

All readers have expectations. They assume what they read will meet their expectations. In your essay your job is to ensure those expectations are met, while at the same time, fulfilling the purpose of your writing.

Once you have decided on the purpose, you will then need to examine how this will affect your readers. Perhaps you are explaining your topic when you really should be convincing your readers to see your point. Writers and readers may approach a topic with conflicting purposes. Your job as the writer of the essay is to ensure both are being met.

44. Purpose and audience

Often your audience will help you determine your purpose. The beliefs they hold will tell you whether or not they agree with what you have to say. Suppose, for example, you are writing to ***persuade*** readers ***against*** censorship of calypso music. Your purpose will differ depending on the audience who will read your writing.

45. Intention and purpose of writing

Writers usually have one or more of these intentions when they write:

- Expression of feelings or emotions
- Exploration of an idea or ideas
- Entertainment or amusement his reading audience
- Passing on information
- Explanation of an idea
- Argument in favor of a point
- Persuasion of his audience
- Negotiation for a solution

46. Identifying Organizational strategies

NB. Do not confuse Organizational strategies with organizational skills (introduction, conclusion, transitions, linkages, formatting, revising, editing)**! Organization strategies are different from organizational skills!**

Organization refers to an understanding of how that author has created the shape or structure of the text. It also includes an understanding of how the author compares and contrast information, how the writer presents problem and solutions, the writer's use of descriptive language, how the author organizes events in chronological sequence, and how the writer uses language to reveal cause and effect. For example, an author may introduce and describe a theory within the introductory paragraph and then go on to offer different points of view in an effort to refute the theory in the following paragraphs. Understanding the organization of the text from the writer's point of view or from the writer's decisions will help you to better understand the text.

- There is a distinction between organizational strategies and language techniques. Organizational strategies are ways in which the text or discourse was organized. For example in an Expository piece the writer may use an ***analogy*** to introduce the topic where he or she compared one element to another.

- In identifying and giving an example of the strategy as given in the passage you must link the writer's use of this strategy with the achievement of his purpose. For example "Another *strategy that the writer used is that of contrast. This can be seen when he discussed the differences between ordinary waves and powerful tsunamis and different types of explosives.(Make the link between the organizational strategy and the achievement of his purpose)* ***By comparing these two different elements the writer shows the reader how terrifyingly destructive,***

vast and speedy tsunamis are when compared to waves. (Paper 02, Module 1, 2010)

- Some students correctly identify the organizational strategy or language technique but ***do not link*** it with the writer's purpose and thereby get no mark for their effort.

- For any organizational strategy or language technique to be effectively utilized in the passage you must write about the connection between the strategy or technique and the achievement of the writer's purpose. Effectiveness is how the strategy or technique is used and how it connects or relates to the achievement of the writer's purpose; it is not just identifying and naming the strategy or technique!

- Some students seem to approach this Module One essay with pre-planned strategies and techniques and as such they create strategies and techniques when there are none.

- A final word of advice "*Do not critique the passage!*" and thus you should not be making statements such as, "*the writer could have*" or "*the writer should have.*"

47. Organizational Strategies

A *writer* can choose a mixture of different organizational strategies and language techniques to achieve a desired purpose or intention.

A list of some common Organizational strategies

- Examples and Illustrations
- Historical data and Facts
- Statistical data
- Definitions and Classifications and Descriptions
- Cause and Effect Analysis
- Comparison and Contrast

Definition

Writers often use **definition** for key terms of ideas in their essays. A *formal definition*, the basis of most dictionary definitions, has three parts: the **term** to be defined, the **classification** to which the term belongs, and the **features** that distinguish this term from other terms in the classification.

Classification

Classification is a form of analyzing a subject into types. We might classify automobiles by types: Trucks, Sport Utilities/ SUVs, and Sedans. We can (and do) classify university classes by faculties: Engineering, Medical Science, Social Science, Humanities, Management/Business, and Agriculture.

Examples and illustrations

Examples and illustrations are a basic kind of evidence and support that are used in expository and argumentative writing.

Comparison and contrast

Comparison and contrast can be used to organize an essay. You may wish to consider which of the following two outlines would help you organize your comparison essay.

Block comparison of A and B

- Introduction and Thesis Statement
- Description of A
- Description of B (and how B is similar to/different from A)
- Conclusion

Alternating Comparison of A and B

- Introduction and Thesis Statement
- Aspect One: Comparison/contrast of one element of A and B
- Aspect Two: Comparison/contrast of a second element of A and B
- Aspect Three: Comparison/contrast of a third element of A and B

Analysis

Analysis is simply dividing some whole into its parts or sections. A library has distinct parts such as a reference desk, archives, children section, study area, electronic catalog, reserve desk, foreign language section, government documents section, inter-library loan and desk. If you are writing about a library, you may need to know all the parts that exist in that library.

Description

When you think of a description you usually think of it using only the visual. You may also use the other senses such as hearing, touch, feeling, and smell in your attempt to describe something for your readers.

Process analysis

Process analysis is analyzing the chronological steps in any operation. A pancake recipe contains process analysis. First, sift the flour. Next, mix the eggs, milk, and oil. Then fold in the flour with the eggs, milk and oil. Add baking soda, salt and spices. Finally, pour the pancake batter onto the griddle.

Narration

Narration is possibly the most effective strategy essay writers can use. Readers are quickly caught up in reading any story, no matter how short it is. Writers of exposition and argument should consider where a short narrative might enliven their essay and make use of this strategy. Typically, this narrative can relate some of your own experiences with the subject of your essay.

Cause and effect analysis

In cause and effect analysis, you map out possible causes and effects. Two patterns for doing cause/effect analysis are as follows:
Several causes leading to single effect: Cause 1 + Cause 2 + Cause 3 . . . => Effect
One cause leading to multiple effects: Cause => Effect 1 + Effect 2 + Effect 3 . . .

Remember that whichever strategy (ies) you identify in your essay you must always show how they help the writer achieve his or her purpose!

48. Some Organizational Strategies found in CAPE Past Papers

- Use of details for introduction or emphasis
- Use of historical record
- Use of eyewitness account
- Use of scientific data
- Chronological sequencing
- Use of humor
- Use of narrative discourse to present or discuss a complex issue
- Use of analogy
- Presentation of an issue in a number of different ways

49. Literary devices

Literary devices are used to improve the effectiveness, clarity, and enjoyment of writing. Authors of nonfiction, fiction, poetry, and drama use a variety of tools to create emotional mood, attitude, setting, and characterization. Literary devices are one of the most effective tools that an author possesses to draw a mood more artfully or to persuade more eloquently.

When looking at literature, you are not only looking at what is going on in the story or poem, or how you are feeling about it, but you are also looking at how the author is conveying the story or theme. Literary devices and terms help you to define the techniques used in any piece of literature.

When writing a critical analysis of a piece of literature, you are first asked to identify the literary devices such as ***metaphors***, ***personifications*** and ***similes*** which are used in the piece. Then you are asked to make a connection between those devices and the theme of the text. Simply put, the three main questions to which you seek answers are: How does the method that the author employs help to create the meaning of the piece? How effective were these devices? Do you believe that the writer achieved his purpose?

- ***Irony***—Writers use irony to keep readers alert—helps avoid predictability, and often leaves an impression on the reader.
- ***Foreshadowing***—Many writers leave clues throughout the piece, despite having an ending that may surprise some reader. An example of foreshadowing can be found in Shakespeare's Romeo and Juliet where both characters spoke of death quite often and eventually took their lives quite tragically at the end.
- ***Repetition***—Saying the same thing over and over in some cases helps to drive home a point.
- ***Symbolism and metaphor***—By drawing parallels between similar objects and concepts, writers create stories to which others can relate.

- ***Mood***—The atmosphere or emotional condition created by the piece, within the setting. Mood refers to the general sense or feeling which the reader is supposed to get from the text. Mood is a *literary element*, not a technique. The mood must therefore be described or identified. It would be incorrect to simply state, "The author uses mood" rather, it would be better to say for example: "*The mood of Macbeth is dark, murky and mysterious, creating a sense of fear and uncertainty in readers.*"

50. How to analyze the effects of the writer's use of examples

- Literary devices are ways to improve *effectiveness*, *clarity*, and *enjoyment* of writing. Authors of nonfiction, fiction, poetry, and drama use a variety of tools to create not only emotional mood, an attitude, a setting, and characterization in their work but, they also use devices to help them achieve their purpose. The achievement of a writer's purpose is very important in that *all writers write with a specific purpose or intention in mind.* Literary devices are one of the most effective implements that an author possesses to draw a mood more artfully or to persuade their audience more eloquently.

- When looking at a literary piece, you are not only looking at what is going on in the piece, or how you are feeling about it, but you are also looking at ***how*** the author is conveying the topic, idea or main point. Literary devices and terms give us definitions for the techniques used in any piece of literature. When writing a critical analysis, first ***identify*** the literary devices used in the piece (images, metaphors, analogies, etc.). Then, make a ***connection*** between those devices and the theme (s) or purpose of the text. How does the strategy or technique that the author employs help to create the meaning of the piece or in this case achieve purpose?

- To write about the effectiveness of literary devices can be a daunting challenge for many students as many would rather identify and write about the definition of these devices and sadly many do just that!

- When writing about the effectiveness of a device you in your capacity as writer should strive not to ***tell*** about the particular device but rather to ***show*** what this device has done to the piece and especially how it has helped the writer to achieve purpose. A few tips to follow when commenting on the effectiveness of devices:

- Don't simply list devices; focus on the required amount and show how and why they are used—what the device adds to the meaning and purpose of the text. Literary devices are not important in and of themselves, and truly excellent writers don't just observe devices, they discuss their consequences. Literary devices are tools the author uses to create meaning via the achievement of their purpose. Ask yourself "*So what?*" If there's a metaphor, so what? What purpose does it serve?

- The following is an example of a comment on the writer's use of metaphor as a language technique:

  The "crystal stair" represents an easy life, with all the way smooth and clear for you to just waltz on up it. When the mother begins to tell her son about how the "stairs of life" have been for her, she describes a dilapidated, dangerous staircase. Evidently, her life hasn't been too easy: she's had to climb on up carefully, avoiding the tacks and splinters. This metaphor effectively shows what she's trying to say and at the same time helps the writer to achieve his purpose which in this case was to highlight

that the mother persona in the poem have not had an easy life but she was not ready to give up. A metaphor is a great way to** "show, not tell" **how the writer's purpose is achieved in this specific example it proves a point so much more clearly and beautifully than if the mother had just said "my life is hard." The metaphor in this poem provides description of exactly *how* hard her life has been

- Literary terms should be used correctly and appropriately. If you're not sure what a term means or refers to, don't use it in your essay, and don't make up devices. Finally, do not waste time to define literary terms. Your Communication Studies teachers are English teachers; they already know them. Instead, focus on explaining how the literary device is being used effectively and most importantly link them to the achievement of the writer's purpose.

Rhetorical Devices

Rhetorical means the language and effects that writers use to impress or persuade their audience.

- **Rhetorical Question** a question asked for the reflective effect of drawing the reader or audience into the piece, but not necessarily needing to be answered.

  Example: Are we going to put up with curfews and being harassed by the police up town? Who cares? Do you think it is right? I don't.

- **Exaggeration** trying to impress or influence by overstating a viewpoint, statement or idea. The writer in many instances uses exaggeration for the sole purpose of emphasising a point.

Example: Millions of students all over the world go home and rush eagerly into their homework in order to secure their future.

- **Understatement**

  As above, but understating a viewpoint for effect.

  Example: A few students will wander home and perhaps turn on television.

- **Contrast/Juxtaposition**

  When the writer puts forward two opposite viewpoints, ideas or concepts are placed close to each other for effect. Similar to exaggeration and understatement close together, words in close proximity can highlight and improve the effectiveness of the writer's ideas.

  Example: Let us rise up! Let us break the chains, shackles and nightmare of slavery and embrace each other in the dream of freedom.

- **Quotations from well-known sources**

  Such as the Bible, television, classic movies, proverbs and clichés which serve to link with the audience and the common, shared experiences.

  Example: Turn the other cheek; an eye for an eye, a tooth for a tooth. Yabba Dabba Dooo; Eat my shorts; It's moments like these . . . . Make my day; I'll be back! Shaken, not stirred. A stitch in time saves nine; a bird in the hand is worth two in the bush. Straight from the horse's mouth

Conscious Use of Personal Pronouns

Speakers and writers both have these in common: they all want to make their audience agree with their viewpoints and disagree with the things they are against. The deliberate use of including or excluding pronouns helps them do this.

- **Pronouns to address the audience** basically to address them as a group, but not necessarily to persuade them at this stage.

  Example: You are here tonight to witness the finals of the speech contest, where ***your*** sons and daughters face up to a great challenge.

- **Pronouns to include the audience**
  Speakers want the audience to be on their side and agree with their statements/ideas

  Example: We came here tonight to choose ***our*** town symbol. ***We*** don't want a clock—Arima has a clock. ***We*** don't want a statue as our symbol—St James and Port-of Spain have statues. Let ***us*** choose our Humming Bird—it's ***ours*** and always will be.

- **Pronouns to exclude the audience or to distance the audience:**
  Sometimes we want to distance the audience from those who have differing arguments.

  Example: So ***our*** elders want a curfew in the so-called hot spots. ***They*** think it is a good idea to have a curfew of 8 o'clock on a school night for people of our age. Let ***them*** have a curfew of 8 o'clock so that ***they*** can be out of the pubs and clubs and home with ***their*** families as well. ***They*** cause more harm in society than teenagers do anyway.

Emotive Language

Similar in effect to use of pronouns, choice of words packed with emotion can influence an audience for or against your ideas, to be with you or against you.

- **Words with Positive Connotation**
  Warm fuzzy words that help to get the audience on your side.

  Example: Imagine the perfect scene, not a care in the world, walking down the street hand in hand with your adoring parents . . . . they head to the Ice-cream shop and you discovered that it was Devon House . . . home of your absolute favourite triple scoop choc dipped ice cream . . .

- **Words with Negative Connotation** these words have the opposite effects to positively charged emotive words.

  Example: From a distance you see them appear, dressed in black, hair like knotted ropes. Their top lips quiver and sneer in unison like Clint Eastwood and Zorro in a duel. They see you and appear to scowl and grunt at each other and point at you accusingly.

Sound Devices

Speeches are normally only meant to be heard once, so the speaker normally tries to make main ideas, keywords and phrases memorable using sound effects and devices.

- **Alliteration**
  Repeating the initial consonant of a group of words for aural effect and memorability

***Example*:** We've all heard of **R**ichie **R**ich, **D**affy **D**uck, **F**red **F**lintstone, **S**ylvester **S**tallone and **M**orris **M**inor, but the latest and nastiest alliterative villain to slam our screens—a cartoon nasty that leaves **L**ex **L**uthor and **D**ick **D**astardly in his dust—is **V**icious **V**innie

- **Assonance**
  Repeating vowel sounds for aural effect and memorability

  Example: laugh, laugh, cackle and guffaw. That Sam-I-am, that Sam-I-am, I do not like, That Sam-I-am

- **Onomatopoeia**
  Where the words used sound like the thing or concept being described

  Example: wind swishing or moaning in the treetops sand crunching underfoot cock a doodle doo! Woof! Woof!

- **Rhyming**
  Words sounding similar that are pleasant to the ear . . . they also appeal because the listener can almost predict a part of the speech.

  Example: chocolate chips, greasy dips and dairy whips these are the foods that little teenagers are made of

Figurative language

Language that creates a picture in the mind of the listener can assist in the interest level of a speech. The listener visualizes or imagines figures, images and comparisons. On the other hand oratorical devices help to make pieces more interesting, vibrant and memorable to the audience.

- **Repetition**

Hammers home a point and make it memorable using repetition

***Example*:** Trust is an important concept in society. If you can't trust friends not to blab your secrets all over school; if you can't trust teachers not to blast you for something that he or she let someone away with yesterday; if parents can't trust you enough to let you borrow the car—how can you survive in the modern world.

- **Parallel structure**
  This is like repetition, except that phrases and groups of words are repeated for effect

  Example: I have a dream. I have a dream that the sons and daughters of former slaves and the sons and daughters of former slave owners will sit down at the table of brotherhood.
  We shall fight them on the beaches; we shall fight them on land and in the air.

- **Listing**
  In order to emphasize important points lists are often used

  ***Example*:** Instead of: this school rule change affects all students, say this new school rule change affects form 1's ; form 2's; form 3's; form 4's; form 5's; form 6's; and even form 7's.

Remember most importantly after identifying and citing examples of organizational strategies and language techniques from the piece you must show how the writer used these to achieve his or her purpose!

51. Identifying the writer's purpose or intention

- ***Read attentively*** when the writer explains what he or she intends to do.
- ***Identify the writer's assumptions*** in order to see what he or she expects us to believe.
- ***Identify the writer's examples*** to consider what he or she suggests about the purpose.
- ***Identify the writer's audience(s)*** to understand what ideas and characteristics he or she imagines that they both share, and how those ideas and characteristics are significant to each member.

52. Stating the writer's purpose or intention

- Clearly identify the writer's reason for writing
- Is he/she guided by his /her goals?
- What does he/she hope to achieve by writing this particular piece?

53. Effectiveness of the writer's use of strategies and techniques

- Does the writer use these in an effective way?
- Are these techniques superfluous or exaggerated?
- Do these strategies contribute to the overall effectiveness of the piece?
- What impact do these strategies have on the audience or reader?

54. Writer's main point or idea

- Must be clearly stated in the requested number of words
- Must be what the writer is saying
- Must NOT be your interpretation or opinion
- Can be located by identifying the supporting details

55. Reading for the issue at hand

To think critically about your reading you need to:

- ***Consider how the writing addresses its main question*** as one of the categories of questions.
- ***Phrase the specific, main question*** the writing is addressing.
- ***Identify subordinate questions*** the writing answers in the process of addressing the main question.

56. Contexts to which a writer may appeal

- ***To appeal ethically***—Where the writer identifies for you, her own beliefs and values and then shows how your argument can be connected to those values and beliefs.
- ***To appeal emotionally***—Where the writer identifies the emotions that you the reader needs to feel in order to be receptive to the message. The writer also makes use of the strategies that will engage those emotions. Emotional arguments are useful when illustrating a truth or presenting ideas in ways that draw on basic instincts for understanding
- ***To appeal logically***—Where the writer relies on reasons which are supported by evidence, and uses logical relationships such as cause or comparison to support her position. Logical appeals are the basis of most academic writing.

57. Effects of the writer's persona on the message

- ***Make note of the writer's point of view*** which could be either that of the first person, second person, or third person. Speculate on how the point of view supports the writer's purpose. If the point of view shifts then speculate on how this change signals a change in your attitude or perspective toward subject or writer.

- ***Make note of the writer's language choices that signal a specific attitude or bias*** toward reader or subject. How do they relate to the writer's purpose? Simply put, is the writer biased about this topic?
- ***Make note of the writer's language choices that signal characteristics*** of the writer's stance.

    - Is the language more formal or informal?
    - Is his or her attitude more negative or positive?
    - Is the perspective balanced, or does he or she rely on understatement or overstatement to make and support key points?
    - Is there evidence of irony or sarcasm?
    - Are there major points to consider when judging reliability

58. Reliability

Reliability of information found on the Internet

- ***Who is the author or sponsor of the page*?** On the page that you are citing, or on a page linked to it, that individual or organization should be identified, that individual's qualifications should be apparent, and other avenues of verification should be open to you. A page created by a person or an organization that does not provide this information is not a good source to cite.
- ***Are there obvious reasons for bias?*** Is there any advertising? If for example the page is sponsored by Ace Track Shoes, you should be suspicious of its claims for Ace track shoes' superb performance.
- ***Is contact information provided?*** If the page is sponsored by a reputable person or organization, there should be some

other way to verify that reputation, such as an e-mail, postal address or telephone number.

- ***Is there a copyright symbol on the page?*** Check to see who holds the copyright,
- ***What is the purpose of the page?*** Why is this information being posted? Is it for information, as a public service, as a news source, as a research tool for academics, to satisfy a personal grudge and therefore denigrates a target, or is it as a way to gain attention?
- ***Can you verify the information*** on the Web page some other way? For example, can you check the page's bibliography (if there is one) or check the information against a source in the library or some other reputable source?
- Finally, remember that ***even though a page may not meet your standards as a citable source, it may help you generate good ideas*** or point to other usable sources.

59. Evaluating sources

Research does not only involve finding sources, but also involves ***evaluating*** sources. No source should be used ***just*** because one finds it. Analyzing and evaluating sources and the information they contain is an essential part of the research process. Every source one looks at needs to be analyzed and evaluated to make sure that it is an appropriate and trustworthy source.

The two main points that you need to analyze are ***the reliability of the source*** and ***the validity of the content***. For the reliability of the source one needs to judge whether the author and the type of source can be trusted to provide good information. To judge the validity of the content one need to analyze if what the source is saying is correct and appropriate. These concepts can be applied to both print sources and electronic sources.

60. Accuracy

The goal of the accuracy test is to assure that the information is actually correct: up to date, factual, detailed, exact, and comprehensive. For example, even though a very credible writer said something that was correct twenty years ago, it may not be correct today. Similarly, a reputable source may be giving up-to-date information, but the information may be only partially accurate.

Definitions of terms

- ***Sample and Population***—A ***poll*** asks questions of a group, arrives at a conclusion which is then applied to a larger group. Those questioned to obtain the data are the ***sample***. The larger group to which the result is applied is the ***population***.
- ***Authority /reliable authority*** on the subject is someone who can be trusted not to enter his or her own personal, political, or scholarly biases into the text.
- ***Reliability*** is the consistency of your measurement or the degree to which an instrument measures the same way each time it is used under the same condition with the same subjects. In short, it is the repeatability of your measurement. A measure is considered reliable if a person's score on the same test given twice is similar. It is important to remember that reliability is ***not*** measured, it is estimated.
- ***Validity*** is the strength of your conclusions, inferences, or propositions. It refers to the degree to which a study accurately reflects or assesses the specific concept that the researcher is attempting to measure or even the question that she is seeking to answer. While reliability is concerned with accuracy of actual measuring of the procedure, validity is concerned with the success at measuring what was set out to be measured.
- ***Credibility*** inspires trust and belief in the reader. You are more likely to accept information or opinions from someone

who is perceived as having the right to give that information based on her reputation, qualification, prestige, knowledge, expertise or experience in the topic.

- ***A Fact*** is a piece of information about circumstances that exist or events that have occurred. A statement or assertion of verified information about something that is the case or has happened. A concept whose truth can be proved.
- ***Opinion*** is belief not based on absolute certainty or positive knowledge but on what seems true, valid, or probable to one's own mind; judgment or belief not based on absolute certainty or positive knowledge but on what seems true, valid, or probable to one's own mind. Opinion applies to a conclusion or judgment which, while it remains open to dispute, seems true or probable to one's own mind.
- A ***belief*** refers to the mental acceptance of an idea or conclusion, often a doctrine or dogma proposed to one for acceptance e.g. your religious beliefs.
- A ***view*** is an opinion affected by one's personal manner of looking at things e.g. your views about the issue of crime in your country.
- A ***conviction*** is a strong belief about whose truth one has no doubts
- A ***sentiment*** refers to an opinion that is the result of deliberation but is colored with emotion.
- A ***persuasion*** refers to a strong belief that is unshakable because one wishes to believe in its truth.
- ***A Bias*** is a tendency or preference toward a particular perspective, ideology or result. All information and points of view have some form of bias. A person is generally said to be ***biased*** if a reasonable observer would conclude that that person is ***markedly*** influenced by inner biases, rendering it unlikely for him or her to be able to be objective.

SAMPLE QUESTIONS FOR MODULE ONE PAPER01/A 1 hour 35 minutes

GATHERING AND PROCESSING INFORMATION Questions 1-2 Read the following scenario and answer questions 1&2

Several daily newspapers reported that "Video games are responsible for violent teenagers" and consequently school violence. A group of concerned youths decided to research this claim to see if it relates to their community.

1. (a) Identify TWO methods that the young researchers could use to gather data for their research. [**2 marks**]

(b) For ONE of the methods identified above in (a), state ONE advantage and ONE disadvantage. [**2 marks**]

(c) *Identify THREE of the following activities the youths would need to do when they conduct their research?*

(i) *They need to interview persons outside the community*
(ii) *Find out if playing violent video games prevented young people from doing well in school*
(iii) *Choose a sample that is a representative of the community*
(iv) *Identify other activities that they can be involved in*

(v) *Find out a percentage of young persons who had been violent in the community*

---

(2) A couple teenagers were overheard arguing over a report by the ***Today's News***. One of them believed that the ***Today's News'*** claim was erroneous and that the young researchers should concentrate only on getting information from their parents. The other strongly believed that the report was indeed correct and it should be used as one of the main sources.

(a) Explain how **EACH** of the sources mentioned above could be used in the research.

(b) Name **TWO** other sources from which the teenagers may collect data for research.

(c) If this article in the Today's News were about teenagers from outside the region, how appropriate would it for use in the research that the teenagers wanted to do?

SAMPLE QUESTION FOR PAPER 02 MODULE ONE

Read the excerpt below and answer the questions that follow in an essay format.

The Great Chief in Washington sends word that he wishes to buy our land. The Great Chief also sends word of friendship and goodwill. This is kind of him, since he has little need of our friendship in return.

But we will consider your offer. For we know that if we did not sell, the white man may come with guns and take our land. How can you buy or sell the sky, the warmth of the land? The idea is strange to us.

If we do not own the freshness of the air and the sparkle of the water, how can you buy them?

Every part of the earth is sacred to my people. Every shining pine needle, every sandy shore, every mist in the dark woods, every clearing and humming insect is holy in the memory and experience of my people. The sap which courses through the trees carries the memories of the red man.

The white man's dead forget the country of their birth when they go to walk among the stars. Our dead never forget this beautiful earth, for it is mother of the red man. We are part of the earth and it is part of us.

The red man has always retreated before the advancing white man as the mist of the mountains runs before the morning sun. But the ashes of our fathers are sacred. Their graves are holy ground, and so these hills, these trees; this portion of the earth is consecrated to us. We know that the white man does not understand our ways. One portion of land is the same to him as is the next, for he is a stranger who comes in the night and takes from the land whatever he needs. The earth is not his brother, but his enemy, and when he has conquered it, he moves on. He leaves his fathers' graves behind, and he does not care. His fathers' graves and his children's birthright are forgotten he treats his mother, the earth, and his brother, the sky, as things to be bought, plundered, and sold like sheep or bold, bright beads. His appetite will devour the earth and leave behind only a desert.

I do not know. Our ways are different from your ways. The sight of our cities pains the eyes of the red man. But perhaps it is because the red man is a savage and does not understand.

There is no quiet place in the white man's cities. No place to hear the unfurling of leaves in spring or the rustle of insects' wings. But perhaps it is because I am a savage and do not understand. The clatter only seems to insult the ears. And what is there to life if a man cannot hear the lonely cry of the whippoorwill (a bird) or the arguments of the frogs around a pond at night? I am a red man and do not understand. The Indian prefers the soft sound of the wind darting over the face of the pond, and the smell of the wind itself, cleansed by a midday rain or scented with the pinion pine.

Source: From "The Land Is Sacred to Us: Chief Seattle's Lament." A Speech by Chief Seattle (Skokomish) in 1854

(a) State the writer's main point in no more than 30 words.
(b) Write an essay of no more than 500 words in which you include reference to the following:

  i. The writer's purpose
  ii. Organizational Strategies and language techniques used
  iii. Appropriateness of the tone and register used

MODULE 2: LANGUAGE and COMMUNITY

At the end of this module students are expected to be able to:

•	Define a language, and language
•	Describe the characteristics of language
•	Know the purpose of language
•	Define dialect and Creole
•	Have a concept of Creole history in the West Indian context (influence of colonisers)
•	Identify the characteristics of Creole languages
•	Identify the differences between Creole and Standard English
•	Identify the points on the Creole Continuum (Acrolect, Mesolect and Basilect)
•	Identify and define registers
•	Identify the attitudes that persons develop and display toward Language
•	Identify types of communication technologies and their impact on communication

Language

Our language identifies us. It is our life, our culture and our minds. Without language we cease to be a people. We lose our identity. Our language makes us. We are our language. Our language is us. Hosteen Bedonie

61. A language and language

A language is system made up of arbitrary symbols and rules (grammar) that humans use to communicate with each other. A language can also be specific to a particular community. **Language on the other hand is the broad term which** refers to the use of the thousands of all such systems as a general phenomenon. **Language** is considered to be an exclusively human mode of communication; although animals make use of quite sophisticated communicative systems, none of these are known to make use of all of the properties that linguists use to define **language**. Although language is primarily spoken it can also be written.

People over the years have attempted to define language in a number of ways. Some examples of definitions include:

- A system for representing things actions, ideas and states
- A tool that people use to communicate their concepts of reality
- A system of meanings shared among people
- A code that members of a linguistic community use to mediate between form and meaning
- A set of grammatically correct utterances i.e. words and sentences
- A set of utterances that could be understood by a linguistic community
- Thought

62. Properties or characteristics of language

The complex nature of language itself allows it to have many properties. A common progression of natural languages is that they are first spoken, and then written and finally understanding and explanation of their grammar is attempted.

Languages live, die, move from place to place, and change with time. Any language that stops changing begins to die and any language that is a *living language* is in a state of continuous change.

Listed below are some of the properties common to almost all languages.

- ***Dynamic***—Language is dynamic as it tends to change through time according to the needs of the society, or randomly. Any diachronic analysis is the proof for the dynamic nature of language.
- ***Creative***—There is no clear cut limitation for the creativeness of human language. Human beings can produce infinite number of sentences or unlimited utterances by making use of finite number of structures in language or rules in grammar.
- ***Communication of information***—Language is used for transference of information and content of knowledge from an individual to another or from one generation to the next.
- ***Interpersonal relations***—Language is the primary source for the continuation of a society and each individual necessarily uses language to be a part of any social group or to build interpersonal relations and rapport.
- ***Verbal and non-verbal***—In addition to verbal signs, human language includes non-verbal signs which we generally name as body language, but it covers more than this. Areas of study like para-linguistics, proxemics, and kinesics analyze this aspect of language.
- ***Community specific***—The signs and codes of language are unique to a particular community. In this respect, the term "culture" is avoided; since a specific culture may not be always homogeneous. However, the term community covers any sort of social group.
- ***Arbitrary***—The nature of the linguistic sign is **arbitrary** in that any symbol can be mapped onto any concept because there is no relation between the signifier e.g. ***chair*** and the signified e.g. ***the chair itself***. Another example of the arbitrary nature of language can be seen in the Spanish word "***nada"***, there is absolutely nothing about the Spanish word

"***nada***" itself that forces Spanish speakers to use it to mean "*nothing*" and yet that is the meaning all Spanish speakers have been taught and memorized for that sound pattern. On the other hand *"nada"* means *"hope"* for Croatian speakers.

It must be understood however, that just because in principle the symbols are *arbitrary* this does not mean that a language cannot have symbols that are iconic of what they stand for. Onomatopoeic words such as "***meow***" "***swish***" "***hiss***" and "***buzz***" sound similar to what they represent.

63. Functions or roles of language

- The first function of human language is to ***allow persons to think or reflect.*** Simply put language allows for ***reflection.*** Reflection distinguishes human beings from animals. As humans we are able to use our reflective powers to both recall good and bad and ensure that we avoid past bad experiences.
- The second function of language ***allows us to be expressive in our joys, sorrows, pain, anxiety, solidarity and frustration.*** Basically this function of language unleashes our emotions.
- The third function of human language is the most important as it is used for ***communicating our ideas, information and our thoughts.*** All these can be communicated in the forms of statements, commands and questions.
- The fourth function of language is that of using it in ***passing on traditions and rituals.*** Through the passing of these traditions and rituals individuals are afforded the opportunity to be recognized as members of a particular community or society.
- A fifth function of language is that it may be ***used as an identity marker***. For example when one listens to an individual's speech one can sometimes identify the region or country he is from, what status he occupies in society and even what type of school that person attended.

- A sixth function of language is that it has historically been used as a ***cultural identity marker***. The language you speak can indicate and reveal a lot of information about your country of origin.

64. Language can also be seen as

Instrumental when you use it to get what you want and to satisfy your needs or desires. As children little intervention was needed to elicit instrumental language from you as you used it to satisfy your simple needs and wants. As you grew older your instrumental language decreased taking the forms of polite requests or forceful persuasion. Appropriate and effective use of instrumental language in conversation, telephone usage, and in writing is important for skillful language use.

Regulatory when you use it to control the behaviors of others or get them to do what you want them to do. Regulatory language may include giving orders or at more subtle levels, manipulating and controlling others. This kind of language is often used in competitive game situation in which there is a rule-governed "right" answer. E.g. *The Price is Right and Family Feud* Television Game Shows. Positive regulatory language is one of the "life skills" that every parent, shop owner, foreman, or administrator must know. The student who is the Prefect or Head Girl or Boy will be called upon daily to practice regulatory language in the exercise of his or her duties.

Interactional when it is used to establish and define social relationships. It may include negotiations, encouragement, expressions of friendships, and the kind of "maintenance" language we all use in group situations. The 'setting', 'joking', 'ole talk' and 'small talk' that adults often do before a meeting begins is also an example of interactional language. Because adults who are effective in building social relationships are most likely to succeed, children need to develop a comfortable awareness of their ability to use language to establish relationships with other people, to work cooperatively with them, and to enjoy their companionship.

Personal Language when it is used to express your individuality and personality. Strong feelings and opinions are part of your personal language. Personal language is often neglected in classrooms and thought of as being inappropriate. Yet it is through personal language that you are able to relate your own life experiences to the subject matter being taught and in so doing establish your own identity, build your self esteem and confidence.

Imaginative Language when it is used to create a world of one's own, to express fantasy through dramatic play, drama, poetry or stories. This use of language flourishes in the kindergarten or pre-school where you can find play house corners, baskets of old clothes, big blocks and toys. Unless it is fostered, imaginative language will rapidly disappear in later years. Its importance cannot be underestimated, especially when we consider how difficult it is for some teachers to get students to produce imaginative work. Poetry, stories and drama are all the result of your active use of the imaginative language.

Heuristic Language when it is used to explore the environment around you, to investigate the unknown, to acquire knowledge and understanding from the many different sources available. Heuristic language is for investigating, for wondering, for figuring out things. It is the language of inquiry and is one of the most important functions of language on the whole.

Informative Language when it is used to communicate information, to report facts or conclusions derived from facts. Informative language is the language of schools and other learning institutions. Educators use it most frequently and require it of their students.

Summary of descriptions of language

Instrumental
Regulatory
Interactional
Personal
Imaginative

Heuristic
Informative

65. Language and identity

There is no question that language is not only crucial, but probably also the single most critical factor in the construction of one's identity. Language does not only identify the specific country, island or region that one comes from but also gives one a social identity. For example in most instances whether rightly or wrongly, a listener attaches not only a country or region but a social status to a speaker from just hearing his use or command of language.

Dialect

"In the classroom we all learned past participles, but in the streets and in our homes the Blacks learned to drop s's from plurals and suffixes from past-tense verbs. We were alert to the gap separating the written word from the colloquial. We learned to slide out of one language and into another without being conscious of the effort. At school, in a given situation, we might respond with "That's not unusual." But in the street, meeting the same situation, we easily said, "It be's like that sometimes."
I Know Why the Caged Bird Sings**, Maya Angelou **(Chapter 29)

66. About dialects

A **dialect** can be defined as any variety of a language characteristic of a particular group of the language's speakers. The term is applied most often to regional factors, but it can also be defined by other factors such as geographical, ethnic, socio-economic or gender groups speech patterns. Some examples of dialects are British Standard English, Cockney English, Trinidad Standard English, Jamaican Standard English, American Standard English and Yorkshire English.

A lesser-known language, especially one that is unwritten or not standardized is also usually referred as a **dialect.** This use of the word dialect is often taken as **pejorative** by the speakers of the languages referred to, since it is often accompanied by the erroneous belief that the minority language is **lacking** in vocabulary, grammar or importance.

In every language the **dialects** distinguish one social group from the next, for example the dialect of the upper class is different from that of the lower class. In most cases the dialect of the upper class in any community is given the highest prestige and that of the lower class is given the lowest.

To most persons who were not exposed to linguistics, **dialect refers to a non-standard variety of English that only the poor, the uneducated and country folks speak.**

A **sociolect** is a dialect that is associated with a particular social class of people. Other speech varieties of include: standard languages, jargons, slangs, patois and pidgins. A **dialect** is distinguished by its particular vocabulary, grammar and pronunciation. Where a distinction can be made only in terms of pronunciation, the term **accent** is appropriate, not dialect although both these terms are used synonymously and interchangeably.

If two forms of speech are so very different that their speakers cannot understand each other, they are called **different languages**; if however they can understand what each other is saying, then they are called **different dialects**.

More about dialect

- Every language spoken has one or many dialects
- Therefore in most cases if not all, every speaker of every language is also bilingual
- Every speaker of every language speaks with an accent because accent is based solely on the way the speaker pronounces the words.

67. Standard and non-standard dialects

A **standard dialect** which is also referred to as a **standardized dialect** or **standard language** is a dialect that is supported by important institutions. Such institutional support may come from government's recognition or designation or presentation of the standard form as being the "correct", "good", "proper" form of a language. This standard dialect will be used in schools, published grammars, dictionaries, and textbooks. As a result of this standardization of a preferred dialect, persons develop either an attitude of acceptance or non acceptance, superiority or inferiority, appropriateness or inappropriateness for this standard form based on their own lived experiences.

A **non-standardized dialect**, like a standard language, has a complete vocabulary, grammar and syntax, but it is not the beneficiary of any institutional support that is needed to place it on par with the standard dialect.

68. Reasons for a standard dialect

- Because many persons within a community will be better able to understand each other if they use the same standard dialect
- Standard dialect maybe perpetuated in an effort by the powers that be to stifle any sense of diversity which in some society is a perceived threat to their idea of national unity.
- Sometimes in the effort to standardize one dialect over another the result is that the group or groups whose dialects were not standardized are excluded from power. Simply put the purpose of standardization may be seen by persons as a way to exclude certain sections of the society from power.

69. Languages are called dialects

- Solely because they are not literary languages.
- Because the speakers of the given language do not have a state of their own
- Because they are not used in press or literature, or are used very little.
- Because their language lacks prestige.

Modern-day linguists know that the status of language is not solely determined by linguistic criteria, but it is also the result of a historical and political development.

Standard English

70. Standard English in the Caribbean

In the Caribbean we use the phrase "Standard English" loosely when we are identifying the chosen standard form over the regional standard form of English. However, even our Standard form has within it a bit of regional influence and as such one is completely correct to use the term Trinidad Standard English or Jamaican Standard English.

The spoken standard has become associated with education. In general the perception is that the higher a person's standard of education the better that person's command of the Standard English without regional and social characteristics. This occurs because the written standard found in schoolbooks does not include many regional or social features and if it does it is not a regular occurrence. This association does not mean that the spoken standard is more correct than speech with regional or social characteristics. However, standard language is perceived as usually more appropriate and acceptable in formal situations because many people have come to expect it on these occasions.

The standard language has the status which comes with social prestige, education, and wealth, the Creole or dialect on the other hand has no such status, its roots lie in a history of slavery and subservience.

71. Characteristics of Standard English

- Used mainly in formal contexts
- Can be delivered either orally or written with the latter being the dominant
- More complex as it contains grammar and syntax

- Wide variety of both regional idioms and pronunciations
- A recognized dictionary containing standardized spelling and vocabulary
- A recognized grammar which records the forms, rules and structures of the language
- A standard system of pronunciation which is considered by the majority of the population as "educated" or "proper" speech
- The official language used in the making of laws and constitutions thus giving it legal status
- Mainly used in public life such as in the courts, churches, and most public institutions
- To translate sacred texts such as the Bible
- Teaching of grammar and spelling in schools

72. Arguments for Standard English as a language

- Standard is internationally accepted
- Standard English is governed by grammar, phonological, syntactic, and morphological rules
- Standard English can be written
- Standard English is the main language used in the media, in schools and public places

73. Creole and Pidgins

A **lexifier** is the language from which a particular Creole language derives the majority of it vocabulary.

These languages were originally held in low regard, often referred to as *broken* or *bastardized* forms of their European **lexifiers**, This view so ingrained that even today it is easy to find many speakers of creoles who do not consider them real languages, but dialects. Arguably many of them are grammatically distinct enough to be considered different languages, though they may lack *standardized* spelling (orthography) and grammar. The main reason for this is that they were initially used for daily communication and did not develop in comparison with non-Creole languages.

The definition of the term ***Creole*** that is often considered most suitable is a language with a pidgin in its ancestry, which is spoken as a native language by the majority of its speech community. ***Pidgins*** are languages which have developed under the circumstances where two linguistic systems collide and merge, but for some reason have not acquired native speakers. This does not imply that creoles are necessarily more developed languages than pidgins, merely that there was perhaps wider dispersal of linguistic communities or some other pressure to abandon native languages in situations of creolization greater than that in situations of pidginization

74. **Creole in a West Indian context**

In the Caribbean context, the term Creole is sometimes quite fuzzy, but, most times Creole language refers to the languages that have evolved as a result of the Europeans who colonized our islands during the period of slavery and beyond. Our unique Caribbean languages therefore, can be mixtures of Spanish and West African, British English and West African and French and all of the other existing languages of our European colonizers.

All of the recognized Creoles of our region have vocabularies that are overtly and predominantly drawn from some other European language. Caribbean Creole languages have continued to co-exist with the European languages that have official statuses in our region. Thus Caribbean creoles are typically categorized as being Dutch-based, English based, French based and Spanish based.

75. **Language experiences in the Caribbean**

Our language identifies us. It is our life, our culture and our minds. Without language we cease to be a people. We lose our identity. Our language makes us. We are our language. Our language is us. Hosteen Bedonie (2007)

The Trinidad and Tobago (Trinbago) experience

- Trinbagonians possess a language of their own and like so many other Creole languages the language of Trinidad and Tobago is neither "a dialect" nor is it "broken English" and it is certainly not "bad language."
- Englishes such as those spoken in London, Grenada, Jamaica, Barbados and all the other places where English is spoken, are all English in their own right. They all have distinct vocabulary and syntax

Like many of the countries in the Caribbean their language was born out of a series of historical contacts and collisions with elements such as the indigenous peoples, trade, war, slavery, the plantation system and colonialism. For example the foundation of Creole language in Trinidad and Tobago is English, with words, phrases and syntax that are borrowed unchanged from African, East Indian, Amerindian, French, Spanish, Portuguese, Arabic and other languages. Trinidad was a Spanish colony until taken by the French and then the British 200 years ago. Many Spanish place names have been Africanized such as *Diego Martin* has become *Dego Martin, Sangre Grande* is pronounced *Sandy Grandy* and *San Juan* and *El Socorro* became known as *Sehwa* or *Sahwa* and *El Seecorro* respectively.

It must be remembered that Trinidad spoke French for nearly one hundred years of its history, and as such there are many French words and French syntaxes interspersed in our Trinidadian language. The well known phrase—*"It making hot*" has its root in the French phrase *"Il fait chaud"*. Several of our folklore characters or spirits have French derived names such as the well known tales of *Lajablesse* or *La Diablesse, soucouyant, Papa Bois, lagahou.* Some other French words in our Trinidadian vocabulary are *bacchanal, balisier, pomme cythere, mauvais langue, J'Ourvert* and *macommère.*

Baiganne, roti, tawa, pirha, sari, bhoujhi, bhoujha, bheti and *bheta* are but some of the Hindi.

The Jamaican language experience

From the early days of the slave trade through the slavery period, English and African languages were mixed (words, grammar, intonation)with few Amerindian (first peoples of the Caribbean) and Spanish influences as well. Because English was at that time and is the language of power, capital, and prestige, most of the words in the Jamaican Creole language have English roots. However, the sounds and many of the grammatical structures, as well as some words, have a strong African presence as well.

Today Jamaican is spoken throughout the country, as well as in neighborhoods of the Jamaican Diaspora in New York, London and Toronto. It is important to note, however, that English is still the so-called "official" language of Jamaica. English is the language of education, commerce, and the institutional world. Because of this colonial legacy, Jamaican Patois or Creole is still considered by many within the country and abroad as merely "bad English" or "slang," spoken only by the poor and uneducated. Language in Jamaica is a class issue.

Creole languages are found all over the world on every continent. Creole emerges when two or more languages come into contact to form a new language a Creole language is born. In the case of Jamaican language its Creole was formed as a result of the mixing of the language of the European planters and that of their slaves, many of whom survived the journey from West Africa. Whenever there is some type of human "upheaval" people are forced to find a way to communicate using bits of the languages of the parties involved thus stimulating the creation of a Creole language. In the case of Creole languages in the Caribbean, the "upheaval" is the past history of slavery. Most Creole languages are based on one language. As with many other Caribbean countries, the African slaves upon arrival in Jamaica were thrown into a situation where the only common means of communication was English which was the language of their British slave masters, or at least a mixture of English. This mixture can be seen in the existing Jamaican Creole. Creole refers to a mixture of African and European language as well as European persons born in the West Indies; therefore it is inappropriate to refer to the language of Africans in Jamaica as Creole. Patois is a term used widely in Jamaica, but patois/patwa can refer to any language considered broken or degraded in the world.

Language in Jamaica today reflects the history of the country's interaction with a variety of cultures and languages from many ethnic, linguistic, and social backgrounds. Apart from the Arawaks who were the original inhabitants of Jamaica, all other peoples were exiles or children of exiles. According to research over 90% of the 2.5 million people living in Jamaica today are descendants of West African slaves brought here by the British. The local Jamaican language is a reflection of a history of contact with a variety of speakers, but the official language remains to be Standard English. The most influential speakers were immigrants from Africa and Europe. Kwa, Manding, and Kru are amongst the variety of prominent African languages apparent in Jamaican history.

When seen on the Creole Continuum Jamaican patois looks like this: Acrolect represent the educated model spoken by the elite, at the other extreme is the Basilect what linguists call "creolized" English, fragmented English speech and syntax developed during the days of slavery with African influences. This is the speech of the street vendors or higglers, gardeners and laborers with little education and finally the speech of those in the middle where the majority of the population falls can be seen as Mesolect.

The perception that English-lexicon Creole languages are a form of "bad English" still persists today. Jamaican patois continues to be considered an unacceptable official language and an informal language not to be used for any formal purpose. Creole speakers are often compared to those speakers of Standard English. The similarity of Creole to English has led Creole speakers to be labeled as socially and linguistically inferior, although Jamaica Creole is increasingly being used in the national newspapers and in other forms of media. There is no standard way to write in Creole but this has not stopped writers from publishing and creating poems in written in Creole such as, dub poetry, reggae music, dancehall music and dialogue in novels, short stories, and plays. In most written Creole modified Standard English is used.

The Barbadian language experience

The history of Barbados is uniquely different from the other Caribbean countries in that unlike most of the neighbouring islands, Barbados remained under British rule from the day of settlement right up until their independence on November 30th, 1966.

There are two very notable influences on the historical landscape of Barbados, one is the English influence, since Barbados was an English colony from 1627 when the first settlers arrived, right up until 1966 when they gained their independence, and the other is the cultural influence of the Africans from the days of the slave trade and slavery.

Geographically Barbados is the first island west of Africa, making it then a vital stop in the slave trade and many West African slaves were brought for the specific purpose of providing labour on the sugar plantations. The African influence goes hand in hand with the influence sugar has had on the island. Without one, there would not have been the other.

It is truly a unique blend for Barbados in that it has such strong influences from those two regions Britain and Africa, and so few influences from anywhere else. Given Barbados' long British heritage and inheritance of the British educational system, it is not surprising that Barbadians use **British English** including in the spelling of certain words (e.g. *tyre vs tire*, *favourite* vs *favorite* and *centre* vs *center*), pronunciations, and vocabulary. As the official Barbados language, English is used in formal settings for communications, administration, public services and written communications.

A regional variation of English, referred by the locals as Bajan is spoken by most Barbadians in everyday life, especially in informal settings. To the foreigner, Bajan sounds markedly different from the Standard English heard on the island.

76. Characteristics or features of Creole languages

All Caribbean Creole languages have elements of **syntax, semantic**s and **phonology**. All of these creoles show similarities to those languages of the slaves from West Africa. As a result of these similarities there are common linguistic features within the Caribbean creoles despite their base language. Some features of English-based creoles in the Caribbean which can be attributed to linguistic differences or a person's perception:

➢ **The most common plural marker 's' in Standard English is shown differently in Creole.**

- Mary and **dem** went out
- Can you look at **these** book?
- We have **plenty** orange on our tree
- My mom bought **some** book for me
- Ben has ten **marble** in his bag
- The market have a **set** of fruit in it these days.

Each of these sentences contains a plural noun, but in Creole there is no **'s'** ending as is the rule in English.

➢ **Creole speakers express possessive nouns differently; the owner is placed directly before that which is owned.**

- We are going to my **uncle** house
- "John, can you bring Mark **shoe** for him?"
- That is the **man book**

- **Acceptable forms of Creole**

  - She sat in **the ants nest.**
  - I love your **flowers garden**.
  - My mother just love **nuts cake**
  - We does cook **peas soup** every Saturday

- **In Trinidadian Creole the habitual action is shown by the use of 'does' before the verb in the sentence.**

  - She **does** talk too much

- **In Creole verbs do not change to accommodate the English rule of subject—verb agreement.**

  - The man walk to work every day
  - The teacher walk to school every day

- **In Creole, speakers use the words 'much' and 'amount of' with any countable and uncountable noun to express quantity.**

  - Look at **how much** mango on the tree.
  - If you see the **amount of** persons who died in the cyclone

- **In Creole, nouns that are always plural in Standard English are used as both singular and plural.**

  - Jenny brought **a scissors** to school.
  - When she opened the door he was holding **a flowers.**

- **In Creole it is very common to place the verb before the noun.**

  - It have mauby in the kitchen.

- Look the band coming.

➢ **In Creole there is a high level of difficulty in establishing '*could have*' and '*should have*' in creole '*could of*' and '*should of*' and pronounced as '*coudda*' and '*shoudda*'**

- The man **coudda** walk yesterday (Conditional instead of Past Tense)
- She **coudda** do better than that.
- You **should of** known better

➢ **In Creole, the future tense is always formed by placing either 'go', 'going', 'going to', 'going' or 'would' before the verb.**

- I go call you tomorrow.
- We going to go town in the morning.
- Jenny going and buy the drinks tomorrow.
- I would come back next week.

➢ **In Creole, the word 'did' is used in place of 'was' and likewise 'was' can be used with any subject.**

- I **did get** here early.
- **The**y was here early
- She was with he all the time.
- We **was** coming home when we crash.

➢ **Some common Creole formations**

- We **eh** going tomorrow. ('**eh**' instead of '**are not**')
- **You eh** hear you mother call you? ('**You eh**' instead of '**Didn't you**')
- **You going** to the market? (Statement formed as a question)
- **Ent you going** to the market?

- Mary **doesn't want no** mangoes. (Double negatives)
- They **doesn't** walk with we anymore. (The Habitual form)
- The house **does get clean** every weekend (The Passive Voice in the Present Tense)
- The house **clean** yesterday. (The Past Tense)
- The house **go get clean** on Friday. (Future Tense)
- Is **wait, we waiting** for the bus. (Present Continuous Tense)
- Wc **waiting** on the bus. (Present Continuous Tense)
- We **was waiting** a long time for the bus. (Past Continuous)

➢ **Replacing the '*h*' with** 'd' **wherever there are the consonants '*th*'. These will include such words as '*there*,' '*them*', *'these'*, *'the'*, *'they'*, *'that'*, *'then'*, *'those'*, '*than*', *'why'*, *'when'* and** 'what' **e.g.** Someone *dere* **have** *de* **new pen** *dat* **my** *mudder* **give me** *dis* **morning.**

➢ **Dropping the** *'g'* **in the Participle form of words such as** *'running'* **becomes '*runnin*', '*jumping*' becomes** *'jumpin'*, **and '*playing*' becomes '*playin*'.**

➢ **The silencing of the end consonant of words such as** '*kind*', '*last*', *'find'*, *'bend'*, *'hand'*, *'band'*, *'mild'*, *'child'*, **and** *'friend'*.
E.g. The *bline* man wanted to cross the street, so the *kine chile* took his *han* to help him.

➢ **The insertion of 'y' in such words as** *'car'*, *'can't,'* *'gas'* *'cattle'*, *'gang'*, *'candle,'* *'Caroni'*, *'cash'*, *'catch'* ***and*** *'cat'*. E.g My sister drove her new *cyar* to *Cyaroni* and she run out of *gyas*.

➢ **Having no verb in the statement** e.g. **John so sick** he *cyar* go to school.

- **The Adjective functions as the Verb and predicate in sentences e.g.** The dog **big**.

- **Using '***can***' instead of '**may' e.g. *Can* I go?

- **Using** *musi* **instead of** 'might be able' e.g. He *musi able to* carry that load.

- **In Creole,** *Calques* **are combinations of words that help to achieve specialized words such as '***hard-headed***',** '*sweet-mout*", '*big-eye*', '*knock-knee*', '*han'-to-mout*", '*male-doctor*', '*female-driver*', '*fish-man*', '*bird-man*', '*red-woman*', '*water-carrier*', "*doubles man*", "*papers lady*"

- **In Creole, repetition of words such as '***holey-holey***', '***big-big***', '***little-little***' is a common occurrence whenever the speaker wanted emphasis.**

77. Arguments against Creole as a language

- Creole is the language of the lower class, uneducated, powerless, country folks, and persons whose ancestors were African slaves in the Caribbean
- Creole is the language of comedy
- Creole cannot be written as there is no consensus on an official written form
- Creole language varies from island to island
- Creole has little or no prestige
- Creole is often seen as 'sub-standard' and 'inferior'
- Creole is stigmatized as a 'bad' or 'improper' way of speaking

78. Similar words used in British English, American English and Creole

British English	American English	Creole
Lorry	Truck	Van
Holidays	Vacation	Holidays/vacation
Cab	Taxi-cab	Taxi/car
Gas	Petrol	Gas
Settee	Couch	Couch
Booth	Trunk	Car Trunk

79. Creoles and their geographical distributions

OFFICIAL LANGUAGES	COUNTRY	POPULAR LANGUAGES	OTHER LANGUAGES
SPANISH	Cuba	Spanish	
SPANISH	Puerto Rico	English/Spanish	
SPANISH	Santo Domingo	Spanish	
FRENCH	French Guiana	French Lexicon Creole	
FRENCH	Guadeloupe	French Lexicon Creole	
FRENCH	Martinique	French Lexicon Creole	
FRENCH and HAITIAN	Haiti	French Lexicon Creole	
ENGLISH	St Lucia	French Lexicon Creole	English Lexicon Creole
ENGLISH	Dominica	French Lexicon Creole	English Lexicon Creole
ENGLISH	Belize	English Lexicon Creole	Spanish, Garifuna, Mayan

ENGLISH	Anguilla	English Lexicon Creole	French Lexicon Creole
ENGLISH	Antigua	English Lexicon Creole	
ENGLISH	Barbuda	English Lexicon Creole	
ENGLISH	Cariacou	English Lexicon Creole	
ENGLISH	Grenada	English Lexicon Creole	
ENGLISH	Guyana	English Lexicon Creole	Arawakan, Cariban, Warrau
ENGLISH	Jamaica	English Lexicon Creole	
ENGLISH	Nevis	English Lexicon Creole	French Lexicon Creole
ENGLISH	Petit Martinique	English Lexicon Creole	
ENGLISH	St Kitts	English Lexicon Creole	
ENGLISH	St Vincent	English Lexicon Creole	
ENGLISH	Trinidad &Tobago	English Lexicon Creole	
DUTCH	Suriname	English Lexicon Creoles Sranan, Tongo, Ndjuka Saramaccan,	Hindi, Urdu Javanese, Amerindian Languages
DUTCH	Aruba	Papiamento	Spanish, English
DUTCH	Bonaire	Papiamento	Spanish, English
DUTCH	Curacao	Papiamento	Spanish, English

80. The Creole Continuum

In sociolinguistics a **language continuum** is said to exist when two or more different languages or dialects merge into the other(s) without a definable boundary.

It is usually the case that there is not one standard variety of the Creole language to which all speakers conform, but that there is a continuum of varieties, ranging from the **least lexifier-like** and often least socially prestigious variety, known as the ***basilect*** to the most lexifier-like and highly prestigious variety known as the ***acrolect***, with several intermediary levels, known as ***mesolects***. In the Caribbean, Guyanese Creole English and Jamaican Creole English are often cited as examples of creoles which are undergoing this phenomenon, while the Barbadian Creole English is said to have virtually merged with Standard British English. In Jamaican Creole, for example, one might hear the basilectal phrase—:

"mi nah call no name" and in a different context, one might hear its acrolectal equivalent—*"I have not called any name"*

The continuum model represents a continuous spectrum of varieties where it is very difficult to find any noticeable difference between the Creole and standard language.

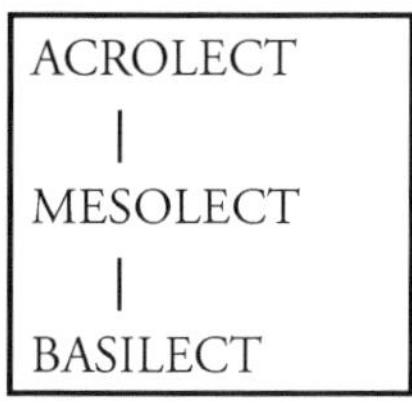

81. Registers

Language Registers can be defined as the kind of language that is appropriate to a particular situation or context. **Registers** refer to the levels of formality or informality and the tones that are correct for a specific context. A **register** can also refer to either the written or spoken language. In deciding what is appropriate for any given situation one has to consider such factors as:

- The **audience** for which your information is targeted
- The **subject matter or topic** that you are speaking or writing about
- The **medium** which can be verbal or non-verbal
- The **writer's attitude** towards the information that he is sharing
- The **purpose** of your communication

Most languages have five (5) registers or language styles. When persons are not familiar with registers they mistakenly treat every situation or person the same way, not realizing one's eventual choice of register is made only after considering these factors.

82. Types of registers

- **Frozen Register:** Used in print and public media, sermons, Pledges, prayers, Preamble to the Constitution for which the reader/ listener is not expected to respond. The language of this register is fixed and unchanged.
- **Formal or Academic Register:** Used in formal social settings such interviews. It is the language of seminars and lectures, ceremonies, public speaking and conversation between strangers. The Formal register almost always involves the use of Standard English.
- **Consultative Register:** Used in situations where the listener is expected to give some form of feedback based on the information provided by the speaker. Examples of this type of register take place between clients and lawyer, doctor, and counselor.
- **Casual or Informal Register:** Used when talking with friends and acquaintances in a non-formal setting. This register is usually recognized by the slangs used.

- **Intimate Register:** This is the language of lovers and persons who are very close. It is also the language that is used in sexual harassment. Usually marked by specialized words or expressions only understood by the parties involved in the intimate relationship

83. Attitudes to language

In this section, the focus is on one-to-one interactions, on how one person might react to others, and they to him or her, based on their language, languages, linguistic variants, dialects and individual linguistic situations.

What is it that you think or what *perceptions* come to mind when you listen to someone speaking a language that is not yours or a 'foreign' language? The feelings that are triggered may be classified as preconceptions, prejudiced—negative or positive—reactions that can have as many sources as there are lifetime experiences. Some of these reactions, if not most, are entirely superficial and subjective. It does not take much reflection to realize how many times one hears someone say, for example: "I hate people from small islands." "I don't like the Grenadians." "German/Germans sound harsh." "I love French . . . it's so romantic . . . the language of love." "Americans can be so bossy." "I just *love* the British accent." There is not even the realization that there are as many 'British' accents as there are regions and sub-regions. Of course "I hate the French," can easily lead to negative perceptions of a French speaker.

Many of the **attitudes** that persons display towards the varieties of English spoken in the Caribbean result from historical, political, social and cultural factors. In most cases people's attitudes are formed from their perceptions of using creole, dialect or Standard English. Their attitudes may range from pride, confidence and celebration to shame, resentment, ridicule and contempt for any choice of language.

84. Code-switching

Speakers of more than one language (e.g. bilinguals) are known for their ability to **code-switch** or mix their languages during communication. This phenomenon occurs when bilinguals substitute a word or phrase from one language with a phrase or word from another language.

Traditionally, **code-switching** has been viewed as a strategy to compensate for diminished language proficiency. The premise behind this theory is that bilinguals code-switch because they do not know either language completely. **Code-switching** was also seen as a sign of a speaker's lack of confidence and pride in one's choice of language or mother tongue.

The notion that people **code-switch** as a strategy in order to be better understood and to enhance the listeners' comprehension is another plausible alternative.

85. Communicative behaviors

This refers to the impressions about the speaker that are communicated to the listener. The speaker may be quite unaware of these impressions. Behaviors can be communicated through a speaker's:

- **Vocalics or paralangue**—speaker's use of the volume, rate, tone and pitch of voice. For example a speaker who delivers a speech at a fast rate might relay to the listener that he is nervous. In the same way a speaker whose speech is delivered in a flat almost monotone voice can communicate to his listeners that he is bored and would rather be anywhere but there.
- **Proxemics**—speaker's use of space as he tries to deliver his message. For example a speaker may stand holding on to the lectern for dear life and never utilizes the space on the stage. This behavior may be interpreted as one of fear.

- **Artifacts**—the speaker's use of objects can also relate a message. For example the speaker who is wearing a tie pin that is the symbol of his country's national flag can be seen as having deep nationalistic pride.
- **Movement and facial expression**—a speaker's use of facial expressions, hand gestures, posture and eye contact in his speech. For example the scowl on a speaker's face can be interpreted as one of disgust.
- **Chronemic**—the speaker's attitude and use of time says something about him. For example a speaker may turn up twenty-five minutes late for his speaking engagement. This behavior may be seen as unprofessional.

It must be understood that communicative behaviors are basically expressed through a speaker's non-verbal communication and may not always be the correct interpretations.

Audience Awareness

To make your communication successful you must have a clear idea of your audience and their interests. For example you should:

- Get the rough idea of the strength of the listeners.
- Think over the age, gender, background and interest of the listeners.
- See whether the audience is patient enough to handle you for hours. Check out if they are friendly or hostile.
- Choose the presentation approach that suits the audience.
- Create a feeling such that each individual feels that you, the speaker are trying to talk with him/her.
- Let the audience know what makes you a credible person to speak on the topic.
- Show your sincerity and whole heartedness for the subject.
- Concentrate on your ideas and do not get distracted by the activities performed by the audience e.g. smiling, whispering.

MODULE 3: SPEAKING and WRITING

At the end of this module you should be able to:

Describe the process of communication
Apply specific communication concepts to different situations
Identify specific features of verbal and non-verbal communication and appropriate contexts of use
Describe the mental and social processes involved in speaking and writing
Identify how specific purposes or intentions and audiences influence speech and writing
Employ appropriate channels/mediums for specific oral and written presentations
Speak in their own Caribbean Standard English on prepared topics using appropriate non-verbal communication cues
Evaluate communication according to set criteria of intention, audience awareness, coherence, mechanics and depth
How to identify the characteristics of advertisements, proposal, speeches, blogs, e-mails, campaigns
Describe the many ways in which information communication technologies (ICT) can be used in the learning process

86. The Process of Communication

Communication is the means by which people generally express their views through speaking, writing, drawing and signing on a day to day basis. You have been communicating from soon after birth through speaking, so you have built up skills and experience in putting across your point of view. Writing was perhaps more difficult, and improved over time. However, your communication skills of both speaking and writing can be improved. Your thoughts, values, views, expectations, needs and concerns must be communicated, or you will not be able to exist. Communicate or die-that is the nature of human beings.

The communication process is the guide toward realizing effective communication. It is through the communication process that the sharing of a common meaning between the sender and the receiver takes place. Effective communication leads to understanding.

The communication process is made up of **four key** components. Those components include **encoding, medium or channel of transmission, decoding, and feedback.** There are also two other factors in the process, and those two factors are present in the form of the **sender/source and the receiver**. The communication process begins with the sender and ends with the receiver.

Sender or source

The **sender/source** is an individual, group, or organization who initiates the communication. This source is initially responsible for the success of the message. The sender's experiences, attitudes, knowledge, skill, perceptions, and culture influence the message. The written words, spoken words, and nonverbal language selected are paramount in ensuring the receiver interprets the message as intended by the sender. All communication begins with the sender.

The responsibilities of the sender/source are to:

- Conceptualize the message
- Encode the message with the receiver in mind
- Choose the appropriate medium or channel
- Transmit the encoded message
- Initiate if there's to be feedback or none
- If and when there is feedback to treat with it

Encoding

The first step the sender is faced with involves the ***encoding*** process. In order to convey the idea/concept, the sender must begin encoding this idea/concept, which means translating information into a message in the form of symbols that represent ideas or concepts. This encoding process translates the ideas or concepts into the coded message that will be communicated. The symbols can take on numerous forms such as, languages, words, drawings/paintings, artifacts, emoticons, pictures or gestures. These symbols are used to encode ideas into messages that others can understand.

When ***encoding*** a message, the sender has to begin by deciding what he/she wants to transmit. This decision by the sender is based on what he/she believes about the receivers' knowledge and assumptions, along with what additional information he/she wants the receiver to have. It is important for the sender to use symbols that are familiar to the intended receiver. A good way for the sender to improve encoding the message is to mentally visualize the communication from the receiver's point of view.

Channel or medium

To begin transmitting the message, the sender uses some kind of ***channel*** (also called a medium). The channel is the means used to convey the message. Many of these channels in the past used to be either oral or written, but currently visual channels are becoming more common as technology expands. Common channels include the telephone, cellphone, the internet and a variety of written forms such as e-mails, faxes, text messages, voice-mails, videos, memos, letters, and reports. The effectiveness of the various channels fluctuates depending on the characteristics of the communication. For example, when immediate feedback is necessary, oral communication channels (face to face or telephone/text) are more effective because any uncertainties can be cleared up on the spot. In a situation where the message must be delivered to more than a small group of people, written channels are often more effective. Although in many cases, oral and written or verbal and non-verbal channels should be used because one supplements the other.

The principal communication channels are *nonverbal and verbal (oral, and written*). Electronic channels—including the telephone, radio, television, electronic mail, and electronic conferencing—employ one or more of the principal channels using technology to augment the channel. Each of these channels has certain characteristics that can either help or hinder communication, depending on the circumstances, the message, and the sender and audience.

Communication channels are often considered from the standpoint of ***richness,*** or the degree to which a channel is able to convey the amount of information transmitted in face-to-face communication. Because communicating face-to-face allows sender and receiver to use and observe nonverbal communication and vocal qualities that complement or contradict the verbal message, it is said to be the *richest* channel, with other channels being less rich as supplemental elements are removed from the transmission.

Nonverbal communication channels include everything that isn't specifically verbal. It includes gestures, facial expressions, posture, dress, clothing, hairstyle, neatness, use of cosmetics, space, time, and paralanguage. Nonverbal communication does not have **advantages** and **disadvantages** in the same way other communication channels do in that other channels automatically include a nonverbal component. Used well, nonverbal communication can increase credibility and help ensure effective communication. Used badly, it can undermine the communication process.

Written channels of communication include such like memos, reports, bulletins, job descriptions, employee manuals, and electronic mail are the types of written communication used for internal communication. For communicating with external environment in writing, electronic mail (e-mail), Internet Web sites, blogs letters, proposals, telegrams, faxes, postcards, contracts, advertisements, brochures, and news releases are used.

In written communication, written signs or symbols are used to communicate. A written message may be printed or hand written. In written communication message can be transmitted via email, letter, report, memo etc. Message, in written communication, is influenced by the vocabulary & grammar used, writing style, precision and clarity of the language used.

If a sender relays a message through an *inappropriate channel*, its message may not reach the right receivers. That is why senders need to keep in mind that selecting the appropriate channel will greatly assist in the effectiveness of the receiver's understanding. The sender's decision to utilize either an oral or a written channel for communicating a message is influenced by several factors.

The sender should ask him or herself different questions, so that they can select the appropriate channel such as:

- Is the message urgent?
- Is immediate feedback needed?
- Is documentation or a permanent record required?
- Is the content complicated, controversial, or private?
- Is the message going to someone inside or outside the organization?
- What oral and written communication skills does the receiver possess?

Decoding

After the appropriate channel or channels are selected, the message enters the ***decoding*** stage of the communication process. Decoding is conducted by the receiver. Once the message is received and examined, the stimulus is sent to the brain for interpreting, in order to assign some type of meaning to it. It is this processing stage that constitutes decoding. The receiver begins to interpret the symbols sent by the sender, translating the message to their own set of experiences in order to make the symbols meaningful. *Successful communication takes place when the receiver correctly interprets the sender's message.*

Receiver

The ***receiver*** is the individual or individuals to whom the message is directed. The extent to which this person comprehends the message will depend on a number of factors, which include the following:

- how much does the receiver/s know about the topic
- how the receiver/s receive the message or their receptivity to the message
- and the prior relationship and trust that exists between sender and receiver.

All interpretations by the receiver/s are influenced by their experiences, attitudes, knowledge, skills, perceptions, and culture. It is similar to the sender's relationship with encoding.

Feedback

Feedback is the final link in the chain of the communication process. After receiving a message, the receiver responds in some way and signals that response to the sender. The signal may take the form of a spoken comment, a return text message, an emoticon via text or e-mail, a long sigh, a written message, a smile, or some other action. "Even a lack of response, is in a sense, a form of response" (Bovee & Thill, 1992). Without feedback, the sender cannot confirm that the receiver has interpreted the message correctly.

Feedback is a key component in the communication process because it allows the sender to evaluate the effectiveness of the message. Feedback ultimately provides an opportunity for the sender to take corrective action to clarify a misunderstood message. "Feedback plays an important role by indicating significant communication barriers: differences in background, different interpretations of words, and differing emotional reactions" (Bovee & Thill, 1992).

Possible problems that may occur within the Communication Process

What are the problems that prevent good communication? Since the process is based on the interactions of two parties, it appears that the problems reside on the shoulders of these two parties.

1. Problems with the sender

A lot of weight rests on the sender's shoulders. The sender is responsible for making all the choices that should incur the highest level of congruity between the intended message and the message received. The sender can make several mistakes from which problems will stem.

Problem: The sender may not know what he or she wants to communicate.

Solution: The sender has to decide clearly what ideas he or she wants to get across.

Problem: The sender does not choose his or her code properly given his or her objectives. If the sender wants to convince a reluctant receiver, the sender should not be yelling at the receiver.

Solution: The sender has to match his or her goals with the verbal and nonverbal tools he or she uses.

Problem: The sender is not centered on the receiver. He or she does not think of the level of understanding of the receiver, of the vocabulary of the receiver, of the cultural experiences of the receiver.

Solution: The sender has to tailor his or her message to the intended receiver.

Problem: The sender is sending contradictory verbal and nonverbal messages.

Solution: The sender should be aware of his or her nonverbal messages.

Problem: The sender chooses an inappropriate medium or an ineffective medium. Each channel has its advantages and its disadvantages.
Solution: Depending on the purpose of the message, different media should be chosen.
Problem: The sender does not pay attention to the existing noises while sending the message.
Solution: The sender needs to try to control as much noises as possible.

2. Problems with the receiver
The receiver is not without responsibilities. In all interactions, the receiver's role will become that of a sender when the feedback phase is reached. So, the receiver needs to pay attention as well.
Problem: The receiver is not listening to the sender. The receiver is not paying attention, is trying to interpret the total message before the message is complete, is trying to judge the sender based on his or her look, is trying to formulate an answer, or is doing something else.
Solution: The receiver should concentrate on listening only.
Problem: The receiver is not decoding the message properly. The receiver does not use the right code. The receiver does not have the same vocabulary.
Solution: The receiver should ask questions to verify his or her understanding of the code.
Problem: The receiver omits to send feedback.
Solution: The receiver should always send feedback when requested to do so.

87. Barriers to communications

The communication process is the perfect guide toward achieving effective communication. When followed properly, the process can usually assure that the sender's message will be understood by the receiver. Although the communication process seems simple, it in essence is not. Certain barriers present themselves throughout the process. Those barriers are factors that have a negative impact on the communication process. Some common barriers include:

- *Noise is also another common barrier.* Noise can occur during any stage of the process. Noise essentially is anything that distorts a message by interfering with the communication process.
- *Linguistic and cultural differences* can create problems for receiver to complete or understand the language used by the transmitter.
- *Environment:* Noise is the basic barriers in the types of environment barriers of communication.
- *Channel***:** A faulty fax machine, a crackling phone or illegible hand-writing can be barriers of channel communication.
- *Receiver's attitude and behavior or mental barrier:* The type comes basically in organization to satisfy clients. It can lead to inaccuracies in the receipt of the information.
- *Transmission journey:* There can be some difficulties during transmission journey. So, it is necessary to repeat the massage and use more than one channel to communicate a message.
- *Lack of planning***:** Purpose to communicate a person should be very clear. So, planning is the most effective thing to void lack of planning in communication.
- *Semantic distortion:* The distortion comes in the uses of words. It may be a serious barrier to effective communication. Semantic Problems occur when people use either the same word in different ways or different words in the same way. An example of this is seen in the CAPE Past Paper question when the owner asked the gardener to "*prune the hedge*" and he eagerly went out and bought boxes of prunes and decorated the hedge with them! The choice of words or language in which a sender encodes a message will influence the quality of communication. It is important to note that no two people will attribute the exact same meaning to the same words

The Noise Barrier

- Noise is any random or persistent disturbance that obscures, reduces, or confuses the clarity or quality of the message being transmitted. In other words, it is any interference that takes place between the sender and the receiver. The effectiveness of the communication process is dependent upon the capabilities of the senders and receivers.
- To overcome the noise barrier to effective communication, the parties involved must discover its source. This may not be easy. Noise appears in a variety of ways from either party in the process. For example the sender may have been trying to watch a television show whilst emailing her friend or the receiver was thinking about what he had to do for an assignment whilst speaking to his friend.
- Have your teacher ever returned an essay to you with comments in the body of the essay that read like, *Irrelevant! Confusing! Where did you get this information from*? Well it is highly possible that at those specific points in your essay you were distracted by some form of noise.
- Once the source, or sources, of the noise has been identified, steps can be taken to overcome it. The noise barrier can't always be overcome but, fortunately, just the awareness of its existence by either the sender or the receiver of a message can help to improve the communication flow.

The Feedback Barrier

- *Feedback* is reaction to any form of communication, without it, the sender of the message cannot know whether the recipient has received the entire message or grasped its intent.
- The receiver activates feedback as he/she returns a pertinent portion of the message to the sender with new information. Feedback regulates both the transmission and reception. The whole process is straightforward: the sender transmits

the message via the most suitable communication media; the receiver gets the message, decodes it, and provides feedback. Feedback also alerts the sender to any disruptive noise that may impede reception of the message. Feedback not only regulates the communication process, but reinforces and stimulates it.

- There is no feedback in a one-way communication. Such a communication involves passing ideas, information, directions, and instructions from authority down the chain of command without asking for a response or checking to see if any action has taken place. It is not enough to ensure the message has been received. For communication to be effective, a two-way process must exist so the sender knows whether the message has been understood. The two-way communication process involves sending a message down the chain of command and transmitting a response containing information, ideas, and feelings back up the chain.

The Mental Barrier

- *The arrogance of the sender may impair the communication process.* If the sender believes he or she knows everything there is to know about the subject being transmitted, he or she expects acceptance of the ideas. If the receiver disagrees with the sender he or she will immediately block out the sender. Communication will not take place.
- *The sender may assume the receiver will respond to his message in a logical and rational manner.* The receiver's priorities, problems, or assumptions may differ from the sender's. The sender might judge the receiver to be incompetent or even an obstructionist. Communication will fail.
- *The sender may assume he is completely logical and rational—that his position is right and must prevail.* This assumption may be false and no communication takes place.

- *The sender may have some misconceptions, self-interests, or strong emotions about a particular idea or approach, of which he is not aware.* However, these traits may be readily evident to the receiver, who may think the sender is hypocritical. This communication will fail, as may all future communications between this sender and receiver.

Word Selection Barrier

- You live in a "verbal" environment. Words constitute the most frequently used tool for communicating. Words usually facilitate communication; however, their careless, improper use in a given situation can create a communication barrier.
- The words we use should be selected carefully. Dr. Rudolph Flesch, a specialist in words and communication, suggests a way to break through the word barrier:

  - ➢ Use familiar words in place of the unfamiliar
  - ➢ Use concrete words in place of the abstract
  - ➢ Use short words in place of long
  - ➢ Use single words in place of several

Perception Barrier

- The perceptual process determines what messages we select or screen out, as well as how the selected information is organized and interpreted. This can be a significant source of noise in the communication process if the senders and receivers perceptions are not aligned.

Jargon Barrier

- Jargon includes technical language and acronyms as well as recognized words with specialized meaning in specific organizations or social groups. Jargon can also be a serious communication barrier. *Newbridge Networks* president Pearse Flynn discovered that jargon was a form of technical snobbery that prevented outsiders from receiving important knowledge thus undermining good relations.

Ambiguity Barrier

- Ambiguous language is usually seen as a communication problem because the sender and receiver interpret the same word or phrase differently. Ambiguous language is sometimes used deliberately in work settings to avoid conveying undesirable emotions.

Information Overload Barrier

- Thank goodness for spam! Can you imagine how many hundreds of unwanted e-mails would have flooded your in-box on a daily basis? This inundation of information is what is referred to as "*information overload.*" On the other hand have you ever been to a seminar or workshop and left feeling overwhelmed because of the volume of information that the presenter tried to deliver in that short space of time? You were suffering from '*information overload*'.
- Information overload occurs when the volume of information received exceeds the person's capacity to process it. Information overload creates noise in the communication system because information is overlooked or misinterpreted when people cannot process it fast enough. Moreover, it has become a common cause of workplace stress.

Information overload is minimized in three ways:

1. You can reduce information load by buffering. Buffering occurs where assistants screen the persons messages and forward only those considered to be essential reading.

2. By summarizing information into fewer words, such as by reading abstracts and executive summaries rather than the entire document.
3. By omitting or ignoring less important information.

Gender Barrier

Research show that there are distinct differences between the speech patterns in a man and those in a woman. A woman speaks between 22,000 and 25,000 words a day whereas a man speaks between 7,000 and 10,000. In childhood, girls speak earlier than boys and at the age of three, have a vocabulary twice that of boys.

Men talk in a linear, logical and compartmentalized way, whereas a woman talks more freely mixing logic and emotion

Interpersonal Barrier

Working on improving your communications is an important activity. Persons need to pay attention to their thoughts and their feelings in an attempt to changing either if there is a need. In this way, they can break down the barriers that get in their way and start building relationships that really work.

88. Forms of Communication

Verbal communication

The basis of communication is the interaction between people. Verbal communication is primarily based on the use and understanding of vocabulary. Some of the key components of verbal communication are sound, words, speaking, and language. Simply put verbal communication has two components: oral and written. The goal of verbal communication is to ensure that the sender of the message and the receiving audience of that message are both interpreting the information in the same manner. This goal can be achieved through the use of non-verbal forms of communication. When appropriate non-verbal communication is used it strengthens the message conveyed by the words.

Written communication

- Memorandum
- Letters
- Reports
- Minutes
- Circulars
- E-mailed messages
- Faxed documents

Oral communication

- Conversations
- Interviews
- Meetings
- Conferences
- Presentations
- Workshops
- Seminars
- Briefings
- Telephone/mobile phone calls
- Audio and teleconferencing
- Video conferencing

89. Non-verbal communication

Verbal communication uses a singular channel, whereas non-verbal communication uses multiple channels. Non-verbal communication involves sending and receiving messages in a variety of ways without the use of verbal codes or words. Non-verbal communication can be both intentional and unintentional and most speakers and listeners are not conscious of this. Non-verbal communication includes:

- touch or haptics
- see or visual
- eye contact (gaze)
- volume
- vocal nuance
- proximity or space (personal or territory)
- body gestures and positions
- facial expression
- hand movement
- intonation
- dress
- posture
- smell
- physical appearance
- sounds (paralanguage)

Broadly speaking there are two basic categories of non-verbal language: non-verbal messages produced by the body and non-verbal messages produced by the broad setting of time, space and silence.

90. The importance of non-verbal communication

Non verbal communication can be used in situations such as:

- When **repeating** the verbal message (E.g. point in a direction while giving directions.
- When **accentuating/emphasizing** a verbal message. (E.g. verbal tone indicates the actual meaning of the specific words).
- When **complementing** the verbal message; but may also contradict it. For example, a nod reinforces a positive message (in the Caribbean), but a "wink" may sometimes contradict a positive message.

- When r**egulating** interactions, non-verbal cues convey when it is the other person's turn to speak.
- When **substituting** for the verbal message especially if that message is blocked by noise or interruption. In situations like these a gesture of a finger to one's lips indicates the need for quiet.

*The adage: "**Actions speak louder than words**" underscores the importance of non-verbal communication. Non-verbal communication removes the barriers that are found in many intercultural situations.*

91. Computerized telecommunications

- Desktop
- Laptop
- Notebook/Netbook
- Tablet
- Handheld
- Software
- Auxiliary Products

92. Communication tools

- Landline telephones
- Cell phones
- Smart-phones
- Video and web conferencing
- Social networking sites
- Online chat tools
- Fax

93. Internet

- Browsers
- Feasibility and specifics
- Internet service provider

- E-mail

94. Auxiliary Products for the computer

Many products can be used in conjunction with your computer to enhance functionality. These also require software specifically designed to facilitate its usage.

- *Digital Camera*—a picture taken by this type of camera can be directly loaded onto your computer for a variety of uses. Usage ideas include pictures of properties, product catalogs, pictures accompanying résumés and many more.
- Digital cameras come in various shapes and sizes, but what really sets them apart in price is image quality.
- *Scanner*—when you have a printed copy of something that you would like to include as part of a digital document, you can create a digital image by scanning the printed copy with this type of equipment.
- *Wireless Transmission*—this feature allows you to communicate with other devices equipped with the same feature. Most office equipment is available in a wireless version and without all the cords. Ease of set up is appealing and has many productive implications.
- Don't overlook the importance of making regular external backups to the individual programs used in your business. Backups are commonly stored on CD's DVDs, USB Flash Drives and External Hard Drives

95. Advantages of communication media

Written communication is able to:

- Provide a written record that can be used for verification
- Provide a medium for relaying complex ideas
- Be used in analysis
- Be used as a contract

Oral communication media is able to:

- See, and hear the sender and receiver
- Allow quick clarification, opinion and views

Non-verbal and audio-visual communications are able to:

- Be used to simplify the written and oral communications
- Be used to provide ideas in number form
- Be used to illustrate techniques

Computerized telecommunications are able to:

- Disperse information quickly to any part of the world
- Transmit entire documents containing text, graphics, photographs via the fax machine
- Conference via the computer allowing for interpersonal exchange to take place quickly
- Achieve a high level of accuracy through these media
- Have or give feedback almost instantaneously

96. Disadvantages of these communication media

Written communications tend to:

- Be very formal, stilted and uncomfortable to some
- Encounter problems with interpretation
- Not allow instant feedback
- Be unable to modify dispatched information

Oral communication tends to:

- Be a bit more difficult to control if a group is involved
- Lack time to sort information out completely
- Be plagued by poor decision making techniques
- Have no written record which leads to arguments

Non verbal and audio visual communications tend to:

- o Be difficult to interpret
- o Be too time consuming to produce
- o Be costly
- o Have problems in storage
- o Be difficult to evaluate

Computerized telecommunications tend to have:

- o Difficulty in managing the high volume of information that is transmitted
- o High cost in all areas
- o Problems in that once the message is transmitted there is no chance of changing the tone e.g. an angry e-mail once sent cannot be retrieved and changed. This can be embarrassing.

97. Landline versus Cellular Phones

It is currently estimated that there are still over 1.2 billion landline phone numbers around the world. In recent years, thanks to the advances in cellular phone technology, homes are quickly converting into cellular only households; eliminating their landline phone number.

To start, a landline phone is any type of phone connection that travels through a solid conduit, typically a cable, wire, or optic fiber. The landline is also commonly called the main line of a fixed line telephone connection.

The following are but a few of the advantages and disadvantages of having a landline phone number as opposed to a cell phone.

The Advantages

- A landline phone number is far more reliable than having a cellular phone. This doesn't mean that there aren't problems and issues that come along with the landline, but using a fixed cable to transfer the call information is far more stable than using a cellular phone, which relies on radio waves to transfer the information.
- Landlines provide a far more stable connection, which leads to clearer calls. With a cellular phone, you can have dropped calls, no bars, poor connections, and static conversations.
- Along with the obvious advantage of having a solid and stable connection, landline phones also provide greater security for phone calls, which is especially important for those times when you are talking about sensitive information like medical records or bank information.
- Unlike cellular phones which can be intercepted by an outside object or individual intercepting the radio waves put out by the phone it is more difficult to intercept a landline. To do so you have to have access to the wire or cable it-self, this is far more difficult.
- Finally, there's the obvious advantage of price. A landline phone numbers will cost far less than their cellular counterparts, based both on talk time and the cost of the initial connection. Landlines cost far less to setup and you will not be burdened with the need to count minutes to make sure you don't go over your monthly allotment. The majority of landline phone numbers come with virtually unlimited local calling and affordable fees for long distance calling. Since the landline isn't going anywhere but in your home, you won't ever have to worry about roaming charges either.

The Disadvantage

- The biggest disadvantage is the lack of mobility. Even when using a cordless phone, you are confined to your home to have telecommunications contact with other people. Once you leave your home, you cannot use your landline phone number.

98. Cell phones

Many people cannot imagine life without cell phones. Many of my students openly share that they can't survive an hour, let alone a day, without their cell phone. Some may think that this is addiction in the making, but for many cell phone users, cell phone has got them connected to their network of family, friends, acquaintances and even Facebook! The loss of one's cell phone can be a very traumatic experience. It is not just the monetary loss; it is something even more, something even bigger. It is a great emotional loss and loss of private data. We may not realize, but a cell phone becomes a part of our physical, emotional and mental life. The minute we are in trouble, we call our friends and family for help with our cell phone. Close friends are always texting each other. Listed below are some of the advantages and disadvantages of cell phones.

The Advantages

- People keep in contact with each other at anytime. Even when you are not at home or are out of the office, your family members or your classmates still can contact you.
- Enhance relationships among people. If you go on vacation, you can keep in contact with your relatives by dialing their mobile phone numbers no matter where they are. The distance will be shortened by talks and sharing.
- The entertaining features afford you the opportunities to relax and surf the internet, logging on to Yahoo Messenger, reading online newspapers or playing interesting games

with other players online. This means of relaxation is extremely valuable for busy people who have no free time to go to entertainment centers to reduce stress from lengthy working days.

Technology and the need to stay in touch have fueled the growth of cellular telephones around the world. These devices can provide voice calling, entertainment, text messaging, directions and web access at the click of a button. However, their pervasiveness and convenience come with disadvantages.

The Disadvantages

- *Cost*: With monthly costs for features such as voice service, text messaging, roaming, and downloading; cell phones can be very expensive.
- *Distraction*: Cell phones can ring in the middle of movies, music concerts, plays and other areas where silence is required, such as libraries, bookstores, hospital rooms and even in places of worship. This happens despite signs and verbal requests. In addition, the glow of cell phone screens from text messages can annoy and distract people in the darkness of a theater.
- *Driving*: Cell phone use while driving has caused so many accidents that many countries have banned the use of cell phones whilst driving except if the driver is using a hands free set.
- *Lack of Privacy*: Because cell phones provide no audio feedback through the earpiece, some people talk much louder with cell phones than they do through land lines. This exposes the people around them to their conversations.
- *No Isolation*: Gone are the days of "getting away from it all." Cell phones make it difficult to remain out of contact with friends and family members. Even if you turn off your ringer, callers can fill your voice mail and your text inbox with messages.

- *Health:* Cell phones emit low levels of RF (radio frequency) radiation. Large amounts of this energy can heat and damage tissue, especially around the eyes and testicles, which do not have enough blood flow to carry away such heat. There is also concern that cell phones might cause cancer, headaches, sleep problems and memory loss.
- *Addiction*: One of the most obvious pitfalls is mobile phone addiction. It is believed to be as serious as drug-addiction, causing a big problem not only for individuals but for the whole society. Teenagers invest most of their time in chatting, playing games, personalizing their profiles, writing texts and neglecting all the things around them. Depending too much on cell phone usage can limit social interaction, making people less active and outgoing.

Technology

The following commentary illustrates new challenges that technology brings to human relationships

"What would you like for dinner?"
No answer.
"What would you like for dinner?" my mother repeated raising her voice. There was still no answer. I look back at my sister to find her staring blankly into space, nonchalantly listening to her iPod. When she notices us staring at her, she pulls her earplug speakers out of her ears and says "Wha?"
This is a common occurrence around my house. Repeating questions two, three, four times before getting any responses.
My sister it seems has her iPod glued to her ear 24 hours a day; maybe you know someone similar. You have an entire conversation with them only to find they've been jamming their favorite Machel Montano's soca the entire time!"
Music fans would probably not hesitate to buy a portable music-playing device like an iPod. These advances in technology however, make

many of us wonder if the future holds a world where communication, particularly face-to-face communication, is becoming obsolete.

More and more technology is breaking through the lines of communication it once encouraged. Inventions such as the iPod and MP3 tend to isolate people, allow them to go into their own world leaving the rest of us on the sidelines as observers. Entering into your own world or even creating your own space is not an entirely bad situation; people need personal time, time to relax, but these convenient little gadgets somehow manage to act as barriers to the everyday interactions that we were once used to.

This isolation is not typical. While gadgets like the iPod and MP3 may isolate users from their family (as my sister above), it may also draw them into another community, a community of iPod and MP3 users.

Today's technologies it seems somehow manage to draw people out of one type of communication into another. Technology creates another environment for them. Trying to talk to teenagers while they are IMing or liming on "MY Lime" is a frustrating venture! It is reminiscent of talking to a brick wall! While the teens may be unable to communicate with you, they can be communicating with an innumerable amount of people on the Internet.

Aside from communication, technology fosters an identity whether false or real. It is now a common belief that one could probably tell a lot about a person by listening to their iPod or their cell phone conversation! This may be right. People use these gadgets, these technologies, to express themselves.

'We are what we eat' went the old adage of the 90's. Today, it can be replaced by 'we are the technologies we use.'

How many people now work from home via their computer? How many people stay in touch mainly via e-mails? How many people text message? How many people are addicted to Instant Messenger?

Some of these activities are all fun but are drawing us away from traditional means of communication and into the new world of communicating via the cyberspace. Everyone is busy communicating with someone. Family chats and family dinners are becoming rare entities and sadly, things of the past.

The key to using technology is moderation.

99. Technology then and now

The **printing press** is a revolutionary communication tool in that it allows large scale one—to—many communication. The Internet is likewise revolutionary in that it allows large scale many—to—many forms of communication.

The **Internet** allows a unique system of interaction in which many people can interact and exchange information with each other. The printing press allowed for only a one-way exchange of information. While a **web site** is primarily a one—to—many means of communication, there are other facets of the Internet such as **Internet newsgroups and blogs** that are many—to—many. Internet newsgroups, which are like electronic message boards where people quickly exchange ideas with one another, are just like an immediately available, instant feedback, constantly updated 3-dimensional book. This further facilitates the generation of new ideas since there is now an exchange of ideas that can quickly be expanded on, as opposed to a single person sharing his ideas and then the public reacting to it over a long period of time. However, there is also a drawback to this many to many system of information exchange that the Internet presents.

Since there is no barrier of entry and anyone can post information on the internet, information overload can become a problem. The extensive amount of information makes it difficult to distinguish useful information from junk information.

Before the printing press, information storage relied mostly on memory and information retrieval on mnemonic devices (tricks that one uses to help memorize something) such as acronyms and acrostics, rhymes, groupings and imagery. This sort of a system seriously limited the amount of information that could be dealt with.

The **printing press** and the **Internet** both ignore the lower income class. The lower income class did not receive much of the direct benefits of the printing press because they were illiterate. They felt the effect in a roundabout way as progress in society affected everyone within it. However, in general the printing press passed them by. The same can be said about the Internet because the lower income classes have little exposure to the Internet since costs of owning a computer and being networked remain high.

Just as the **printing press** initially created a literate middle class, a class division may also be created around computer literacy. Those persons who are computer literate have an advantage over those who are not in all sectors of society today, which is nearly as great as the advantage the literate middle class had over the illiterate lower class. Those who are computer literate are more likely to succeed. Thus they will continue to be able to afford computer and internet access in future generations. It is possible that persons who are computer illiterate will not have the marketable skills necessary to bring them the income required to have sufficient access to computers and the internet. In this way a disadvantaged underclass of the computer illiterate may form. However, the availability of internet cafes with their relatively low hourly rates will facilitate in the future greater use of technology by the lower income groups.

100. Communicating then and now

The typical person that lived before the dawn of the Information Age of the 20th Century existed with a totally different mindset. Such an individual had a very distinct way to communicate. When people communicated over long distances, they waited patiently and expected delays in messages. No one really seemed to be in a hurry to do things or was too busy to stop and chat with another person. Opening letters and hearing people's voices was an integral part of their lifestyle and ideas were shared in person or face-to-face. Everyone knew the face behind the person to whom they spoke, and people enjoyed long conversations over meals and visiting others in person and their styles of communication did not depend on communication technologies too greatly.

After the advent of the telephone, cell-phone and Internet, communication technologies became a more integral part of everyday life and just as with everything in this world these too have their advantages and disadvantages. New technology such as the Internet has impacted both ethically and unethically on communication practices.

101. Advantages and Disadvantages of the Internet

The internet is a collection of various services and resources. Although, many people still think e-mail and World Wide Web as the principle constituents of internet, there is lot more in store than e-mail, chat rooms, celebrity web sites and search engines. It also became the best business tool of modern scenario. Today internet has brought the entire world in a single room. From news across the corner of the world, wealth of knowledge to shopping, purchasing the tickets of your favorite movie-everything is at your finger tips. Internet has great potential and lot to offer . . . however, like every single innovation in science and technology, internet has its own advantages and disadvantages.

Advantages of the internet

- *Communication*: The main focus of internet has always been the communication. And internet has excelled beyond the expectations. Still; innovations are going on to make it faster, more reliable. By the advent of computer's Internet, our earth has reduced and has attained the form of a "*global village*".

  Now we can communicate in a fraction of second with a person who is sitting in the other part of the world. Today for better communication, we can avail the facilities of e-mail, Messenger and Skype we can chat for hours with our loved ones. There are plenty messenger services in offering. With help of such services, it has become very easy to establish a kind of global friendship where you can share your thoughts, can explore other cultures of different ethnicity.

- *Information*: Information is probably the biggest advantage internet is offering. The Internet is a virtual treasure trove of information. Any kind of information on any topic under the sun is available on the Internet. The search engines like Google, Yahoo, MSN and Firefox is at your service on the Internet. You can almost find any type of data on almost any kind of subject that you are looking for. There is a huge amount of information available on the internet for just about every subject known to humankind, ranging from academic subjects, government law and services, parties and conferences, market information, tourist travel information, new ideas and technical support, the list is endless.

  Students and children are among the top users who surf the Internet for research. Today, it is almost required that students should use the Internet for research for the purpose of gathering resources. Teachers have started giving assignments that require research on the Internet. For example, numerous web sites available on the net are offering loads of information for people to research diseases and talk to doctors online at sites such as, America's Doctor

- *Entertainment*: Entertainment is another popular reason why many people prefer to surf the Internet. In fact, media of internet has become quite successful medium that offers multifaceted entertainment factor. Downloading games, visiting chat rooms or just surfing the Web are some of the uses people have discovered. There are numerous games that may be downloaded from the Internet for free. The industry of online gaming has tasted dramatic and phenomenal attention by game lovers. Chat rooms are popular because users can meet new and interesting people. In fact, the Internet has been successfully used by people to find lifelong partners. When people surf the Web, there are numerous things that can be found. Music, hobbies, news and more can be found and shared on the Internet.

- *Services*: Many services are now provided on the internet such as online banking, job seeking, purchasing tickets for your favorite movies, guidance services on array of topics engulfing the every aspect of life, and hotel reservations. Often these services are not available off-line and can cost you more.

- *E-Commerce*: E-commerce is the term or concept used for any type of commercial or business deals that involves the transfer of information across the globe via Internet. It has become a phenomenon associated with any kind of shopping for almost anything. Sites such as Amazon and e-Bay are but two of these e-commerce sites. E—commerce caters to virtually every need that a person can have.

Disadvantages

- *Theft of Personal information*: If you use the Internet, you may be facing grave danger as your personal information such as name, address, credit card number etc. can be accessed by other culprits to make your problems worse.

- *Spamming*: Spamming refers to sending unwanted e-mails in bulk, which provide no purpose and needlessly obstruct the entire system. Such illegal activities can be very frustrating for you, and so instead of just ignoring it, you should make an effort to try and stop these activities so that using the Internet can become that much safer.

- *Virus threat*: Virus is nothing but a program which disrupts the normal functioning of your computer systems. Computers attached to internet are more prone to virus attacks and they can end up into crashing your whole hard disk, causing you considerable headache.

- *Pornography*: This is perhaps the biggest threat related to students' healthy mental life. A very serious issue concerning the Internet. There are thousands of pornographic sites on the Internet that can be easily found and can be a detrimental factor to letting children use the Internet.

- When conducting research you can often be led into following non productive searches

- Decreased face to face communication and the ability for persons to adopt false identities

- No process to check information for accuracy

- Web addresses change and sites disappears regularly

- The anonymity and vast reach of the Internet has afforded some persons new opportunity to behave in immoral, unethical and illegal ways. E.g. some persons have fallen prey to sexual predators while interacting on the internet.

- The lack of governing bodies have allowed persons with the propensity to break copyright laws and intellectual property laws and copy music CDs and hack into computers and steal information without being detected

- *Cyber-Bullying:* Cyber bullying is bullying through email, instant messaging (IMing), chat room exchanges, Web site posts, or digital messages or images send to a cellular phone or personal digital assistant (PDA) (Kowalski et al. 2008). Cyber bullying, like traditional bullying, involves an imbalance of power, aggression, and a negative action that is often repeated. Examples of cyber-bullying are:

    - *Harassment*: repeatedly sending offensive, rude and insulting messages to others

- *Denigration*: distributing information about others that is derogatory and untrue via the various means of the internet such as posting on a Web page, through e-mails or instant messaging or digitally altered photographs
- *Flaming*: online "fighting" using electronic messages with angry, vulgar language
- *Impersonation*: breaking in or hacking into someone's email or social networking account and using that person's online identity to send or post vicious or embarrassing material to/about others
- *Outing and Trickery*: sharing someone's secrets or embarrassing information or tricking someone into revealing secrets or embarrassing information and forwarding it to others
- *Cyber-stalking*: repeatedly sending messages that include threats of harm or are highly intimidating, or engaging in other online activities that make a person afraid for his or her safety (depending on the content of the message, it may be illegal).

102. Social Networking

Social networking is the process of finding friends and of managing friendships through the internet. People who wish to meet others on line put up their most compelling and attractive presentations through their profile pages. They join groups and communicate with others by commenting on topics or by introducing topics that hope to encourage discussion.

Social network sites like *Facebook, MySpace, Twitter and LinkedIn* provide more than just a way to beat loneliness or chat with friends. These networks provide wide-ranging benefits from improved communication skills and a more open worldview to a more intuitive way of understanding technology and establishing better relationships with business partners, customers and clients.

- *Social Skills*: For some people, especially the young crowd, social interaction can be awkward and difficult. Using social networks over the internet allow people to improve their interactive personal skills, build friendships and create bonds. Shared interests and hobbies allow people to explore their individuality and always find a circle of understanding friends to feel at ease with or to learn about new ways of looking at situations. These social skills can be transferred to face-to-face interactions as well.
- *Technical Skills*: To maneuver the vast number of pages, updates and links of social networking sites, you have to learn to use the technology. Teenagers have become experts at texting updates to social sites using the tiny keypads on phones. The increasing age demographics on Facebook mean that more adults and seniors are getting online and learning new skills as well. Social networking boosts technical knowledge across the board, giving all users better skills to use in future jobs and projects.
- *Open to Diversity*: The internet is filled with different viewpoints and opinions. Sooner or later, you will come up against information that casts your personal world in a new light. Social networks are hot spots for debating issues, sharing life experiences and getting a first-person look into someone else's world, thus providing for expanded horizons and a wider tolerance of different beliefs.
- *Business Networking and Service*: Social networking provides many benefits to businesses, from finding new colleagues and expanding your professional contacts on LinkedIn to helping customers with issues over Twitter or Facebook. Connecting with clients and customers via social media can bring better, faster resolution to problems and positive word-of-mouth advertising when compared to leaving people to wrangle with automated phone systems and slow response times.

- *Collective Thinking*: For companies that have many employees or a telecommuting workforce, social networking can be a great place to connect with new ideas, share information and give all employees the same tools and goals so that everyone pushes toward success in the same direction. This type of collective thinking can also help keep up morale since everyone can participate. In a more traditional meeting setting, all opinions or ideas might not be heard.
- *Staying connected with friends*: Social networking is the easiest way to stay in touch with old friends, friends who don't live close to you or even just roommates.
- *For means of communication*: Everyone has those days when they wake up without a phone or any way to communicate with the world except through social networking. You could update your social networking profile, and one of your "followers" could even help you locate your phone.
- *Keeping up-to-date on news more quickly*: Some social networking sites constantly update news information. This enlightens readers and social networking profile owners.
- *Achieving a more personal connection*: Having a social networking profile allows you to keep informed on recent happenings with people in your network. You have something to discuss with your co-workers and friends and even an opportunity to do a little brown-nosing to your boss about his most recent personal achievement.
- *Making friends with similar interests and "likes"*: Various social networking sites are centered on certain interests and topics. For example, Flickr is a social networking site that allows its users to upload and share photographs. Creating a social networking profile with these sites would be a fun and engaging way to make friends.
- *Networking*: In today's world, it is not about what you know, but who you know. Having a social networking profile allows users to make and maintain social and business connections.

- *For free advertising*: Social networking profiles allow users to post anything and everything to the virtual world and can be seen by anybody. Having a profile allows more chances for exposure and opportunities for marketing your work and yourself.
- *For creative expression*: The Internet offers a virtual canvas for all users; however, users with social networking profiles could have a more defined group of followers to increase exposure.
- *Experience global exposure:* The Internet has massively decreased the size of the world. This has made the flow of ideas and information an easier process. With a social networking profile, you can be ahead of and potentially influence the next global trend.
- *Creating a positive impact on the world*: Social networking allows users to band together and create strong alliances for a certain cause such as *Child Abuse, Modern day Slavery, Helping Haiti*. These sites allow you to be a virtual part of change in the world and fight for your cause.

103. Cultural differences in non-verbal communications

Appearance and Dress

Nearly all cultures are concerned about how they look and are judged by the externals such as looks and dress. Many western cultures, for instance, appear almost obsessed with dress and personal attractiveness. Study some cultures and note the ways they use dress as a sign of status.

Body Movement

There are more than 700,000 possible motions we can make—so it is impossible to categorize them all. Just becoming aware of the body movement and position is a key ingredient in sending or receiving messages.

Posture

Did you know that?

- Bowing in USA is generally not done or is criticized if done but is acceptable in Japan as it shows respect.
- In many areas in Northern Europe a slouching posture is considered rude
- Having your hands in your pocket is a sign of disrespect in Turkey
- In Ghana and Turkey sitting with your legs crossed is very offensive.
- Showing soles of your feet is a highly offensive act in Thailand and Saudi Arabia

Gestures

Cataloging the variety of gestures is an impossible task. Gestures that are acceptable in one's own culture may be offensive in another. Also the amount of gesturing varies from culture to culture. Some cultures like the Trinidadian and West Indians are animated and others like the English are known to be a bit restrained. Restrained cultures often feel animated cultures lack manners and overall restraint. Animated cultures often feel restrained cultures lack emotion or interest.

Even the simple things such as using one's hands to point and count vary from culture to culture. For example it is very common and acceptable to see persons in the Caribbean pointing with their index finger but in Germany they point with the little finger and the Japanese point with their entire hand. In fact pointing with the index finger is considered to be rude in most Asian cultures.

Whilst gesturing with the middle finger in the Western world is offensive, in Indonesia the middle finger is used to indicate the number (1) one when counting.

Facial Expressions

While some say that facial expressions are identical, the meanings attached to them differ from culture to culture. Majority opinion is that these do have similar meanings world-wide with respect to smiling, crying, or showing anger, sorrow, or disgust. However, the intensity varies from culture to culture. Note the following:

- Many Asian cultures suppress facial expression as much as possible.
- In many Mediterranean (Latino / Arabic) cultures men exaggerate grief or sadness while most Western men hide their grief or sorrow.
- Some see an "animated" expression as a sign of a lack of control.
- Too much smiling is viewed as a sign of shallowness and deceit.
- Women in most cultures smile more than men.

Eye Contact and Gaze

In North America eye contact indicates: degree of attention or interest, influences attitude change or persuasion, regulates interaction, communicates emotion, defines power and status, and has a central role in managing impressions of others.

- Many western cultures see direct eye contact as positive and it is quite common to hear elders advising children to "look a person in the eyes" when communicating.
- Arabic cultures make prolonged eye-contact as they believe it shows interest and helps them measure the sincerity of the other person. Any person who doesn't reciprocate is seen as untrustworthy.
- Japan, Africa and Latin cultures avoid eye contact to show respect.

Touch

Questions: Why do we touch others when we speak? Where do we touch? And what meanings do we assign when someone else touches us?

> ***Scenario:*** *Andy, an Afro—Trinidadian male goes into a mini mart that was recently bought over by new Korean immigrants. He gives a $20 bill for his purchase to Mrs. Cho who is the cashier and waits for his change. He is upset when his change is put down on the counter in front of him instead of in his outstretched hand. "That woman is so rude and does not want to even touch my hand! But she wants my money! Well that is the last time I am buying from her." he thinks as he walks off.*
>
> ***The problem:*** *Traditional Korean and many other Asian countries do not touch strangers, especially if they are members of the opposite sex. On the other hand the Caribbean person has no problem touching strangers and may interpret Mrs. Cho's behavior as an example of discrimination. She does not want to touch him because he is black.*

Response: Each culture has a clear concept of what parts of the body one may not touch. The basic message behind a touch can be that of affection or control, protection, support or disapproval.

- In North America—handshake is common (even for strangers). Hugs and kisses for those of opposite gender or of family are also common and acceptable. Most African Americans touch on greeting but are annoyed if touched on the head as this is perceived to having the 'good boy, good girl overtones' that is belittling.
- Persons in Islamic and Hindu cultures typically do not touch with the left hand. To do so is a social insult. Left hand is for toilet functions.

- Many Islamic cultures generally do not approve of any touching between genders (even handshakes). But consider such touching (including hand holding and hugs) between same-sex to be appropriate.
- Many Asians don't touch the head because for them the head houses the person's soul and a touch puts that person in jeopardy.

Body odors

- In many western countries there is a fear of natural smells such as sweat or perspiration and as such there is a billion dollar industry to mask objectionable odors with what is perceived to be pleasant odors such as deodorants, air fresheners and disinfectants.
- Many other cultures consider natural body odors as normal for example the Arabic culture.

Asian cultures such as the Filipino, Malay, Indonesian, Thai, and Indian stress frequent bathing—and often criticize other cultures for not bathing often enough.

104. Paralanguage

- Vocal qualities such as a laugh, cry, yell, moan, whine, belch, and yawn send different messages in different cultures. For example in Japan one's giggling is seen as a sign of embarrassment and in India to belch loudly after a meal is an indication of your total satisfaction with the meal.
- Loudness indicates strength in Arabic cultures and softness indicates weakness; to the Japanese loudness is an indication that you have lost control of the situation. Generally, one learns not to "shout" in Asian culture.
- Vocal admissions such as "*un-huh, shh, uh, ooh, mmmh, humm, eh*" normally indicate formality, acceptance, assent, uncertainty.

105. Conscious non-verbal communication

Conscious non-verbal communications:

- Senders of conscious non-verbal communications are aware that they are sending a message and the general meaning of that message. For example the individual hugging another individual knows that she is embracing someone and that that action is normally perceived as a sign of affection.

- Receivers of conscious non-verbal communications are aware that they received the message and the meaning intended by the sender. The receiver of the hug, for example, generally realizes that the message is a sign of friendship.

106. Subliminal non-verbal communication

Subliminal messages are communicated to the subconscious mind of the receiver. Receivers of subliminal messages are not consciously aware of the message. However, these messages are important.

- Gutreactionsarefrequentlybaseduponaperson'ssubconscious reading of subliminal non-verbal communication.
- For most persons, uniformed members of the police, army or protective services subliminally communicate the authority of those wearing them.
- Likewise, well dressed executives project an air of success.

Often, subliminal messages influence the receiver more powerfully than conscious non—verbal communications.

107. Interpreting non-verbal communications

Typically, non-verbal messages are difficult to accurately interpret in isolation because most messages have several possible meanings.

For example, a person's yawn may indicate to one person boredom and to tiredness to another, or both. On the other hand a person's inability to make and hold eye contact with another person might indicate deceit or just plain nervousness.

A non-verbal message is easiest to interpret when it is consistent with other messages that are being sent at the same time. For example, a person might more likely to interpret the person's avoidance of making eye contact as an indication of dishonesty if the person is sweating and agitated at the same time.

108. Non verbal indicators of positive attitudes

Interest in what a speaker is saying can be shown by:

- Tilting head toward the speaker
- Sitting forward in your seat
- Nodding your head
- Eyes focused on the speaker

Confidence is often shown by:

- Hands in your pocket with your thumbs outside
- Fingers joined in a steeple position
- Hands on your hips

Eagerness in what you are hearing is shown by:

- Rubbing your hands together
- Smiling expressively
- Quickly nodding your head

Respect and **honesty** can be shown by:

- Steady eye contact with the audience or listener

109. Non verbal indicators of negative attitudes

A **defensive** person shows it by:

- Arms crossed tightly on your chest
- Sitting with your legs crossed
- Pointing at the other with your index finger

Deception and **dishonesty** are shown by:

- Frequent blinking of your eyes
- Shifting your focus
- Frequent nervous coughing

An **insecure** person shows it by:

- Fidgeting
- Coughing
- Biting your fingernails
- Wringing of your hands
- Chewing or nibbling on your fingernails

Boredom with a speaker is shown by:

- No eye contact with the speaker
- Your head in your hand
- Slouching posture
- Preoccupied expression
- Yawning
- Glancing at your watch
- Playing with your cell phone

A **frustrated** person shows it by:

- Tightening or clenching of fists and jaws
- Rubbing the back of your neck
- Eyebrows drawn together

- Frantic pacing back and forth
- "Steupsing" (Caribbean)

110. Audio Visuals

The terms visual and audio-visual aid refer to anything that can be used visually to help facilitate communication when interacting with others.

Why use Visual Aids?

According to Edgar Dale in his 1946 theory of the Cone of Experience, the average person will remember about 70% of a verbal presentation three hours later and as little as 10% three days later. However, with a visual presentation 85% is remembered three hours later and up to 20% after three days. Most people's preferred learning style is visual and as such they need to visualize what they are hearing.

Some presenters are uncomfortable with the range of new audio visual technologies that are out there. Given below is a list of some of the basic Audio Visual Presentation Equipment:

- LCD Projectors
- Overhead Projectors
- TV and Video
- Projection Screens
- AV Trolleys
- Microphones, CD Radio Cassette players, Remote controls, Pointers
- Computer Based Displays: These can be on your laptop and presented via data projectors.
- Models: these can be particularly helpful in the case of buildings and other fixed structures.
- Photographs: these can be passed around your audience or displayed by the agent.

- Drawings: Can show details and draw attention to specific items that need to be emphasized.
- Chalkboards and Whiteboards
- Flipcharts and Flashcards
- Posters

111. Functions or uses of Visual aids

- Visually reinforce the points made verbally in your presentation
- To make your presentation interesting
- To enhance the audience's memory
- To summarize the point you will make, as well as those you have already made
- To visually clarify important concepts and analogies

Visual aids are only aids that are meant to add a visual dimension to the points that the presenter made orally. The points made in the visual are intended to reinforce the points made by the presenter.

112. Contexts in which Visual aids can be used

Blackboards/Whiteboards

- Used for spontaneous presentations when no other media is available.

Flip Charts

- Used for small groups.
- Used to show your summaries
- Used to reinforce the groups' contributions.

Overhead Transparencies

- Used for displaying charts and graphs.

- Enable high visibility in large groups.

Videotapes and Films

- When demonstrating a process.
- *When presenting testimonials.*

Using film or video to enhance written or spoken presentations

- A video presentation of any piece will enhance it especially in the area of clearing up 'fuzziness' of words, phrases and situation.

- A video presentation also produces a variety of situations, voices and accents.

- The readers or listeners in this situation become viewers who can now see the presentation instead of visualizing with the minds eyes, as the information can now be graphically illustrated.

- Camera alters the meaning of the situation that is being photographed.

113. Guidelines for use of Audio Visuals

- Some advantages of **overhead transparencies** are that they are inexpensive, easy to prepare and very effective for groups of five or more.
- When using transparencies ensure that the lettering is neat and large enough to be read at a distance.
- Use color to emphasize key elements.
- Limit the number of points on each transparency to one.
- When using media such as slides, video and films the presenter should ensure that he or she checks the venue to locate switches and sockets. The media should be up to date. Load and advance tape or film. Have a backup plan should the equipment fail.

114. Advertisements

Advertisements are the paid, public, non-personal announcements of a persuasive message by an identified sponsor; the non-personal presentation or promotion by a firm of its products to its existing and potential customers.

The **persuasive strategies** used by advertisers who want you to buy their product can be divided into three categories: **pathos, logos,** and **ethos**. **Pathos** makes an appeal to emotion. For example, an advertisement using **pathos** will attempt to evoke an emotional response in the consumer. Sometimes, it is a positive emotion such as happiness: *an image of people enjoying themselves while drinking Coke.* Other times, advertisers will use negative emotions such as pain: *a person having hair problems after buying the "wrong" hair product.* **Pathos** can also include emotions such as fear and guilt:

images of disaster stricken Haiti after the earthquake persuade you to send money.

Logos makes an appeal to logic or reason.
For example an advertisement using **logos** will give you the evidence and statistics you need to fully understand what the product does. The **logos** of an advertisement will be the "straight facts" about the product: *One glass of Trinidad Orange Juice contains 75% of your daily dosage of Vitamin C.*

Ethos makes an appeal to credibility or character.
For example an advertisement using **ethos** will try to convince you that the manufacturer of the product is more reliable, honest, and credible; therefore, you should buy its product. **Ethos** often involves statistics from reliable experts, such as *nine out of ten dentists agree that Sensodyne is the better than any other brand of toothpaste on the market* or One million households are using Magic Jack. Often, a celebrity endorses a product to lend it more credibility: Shurwayne Winchester and Beenie Man *all use B-Mobile.*

Advertising appeals are intended in a way so as to build a beneficial picture in the individuals who use specific goods. Advertising and marketing companies use various forms of promoting appeals to influence the obtaining selections of folks.
The most important types of advertising appeals include emotional and rational appeals. Emotional appeals are often effective for the youth while rational appeals work well for products directed towards the older generation. Here are just some of the various different kinds of advertising appeals seen in the media today:

- **Emotional Appeal**

An emotional appeal is related to an individual's psychological and social needs for purchasing certain products and services. Many consumers are emotionally motivated or driven to make certain purchases. Advertisers aim to cash in on the emotional appeal and this works particularly well where there is not much difference between multiple product brands and its offerings. Emotional appeal includes personal and social aspects.

- **Personal Appeal**

Some personal emotions that can drive individuals to purchase products include safety, fear, love, humor, joy, happiness, sentiment, stimulation, pride, self esteem, pleasure, comfort, ambition, nostalgia etc.

- **Social Appeal**

Social factors cause people to make purchases and include promising to enhance buyers' recognition, respect, involvement, affiliation, acceptance, status and approval.

- **Fear Appeal**

Fear is also an important factor that can have incredible influence on individuals. Fear is often used to good effect in advertising and marketing campaigns of beauty and health products including insurance. Advertising experts indicate that using moderate levels of fear in advertising can prove to be effective.

- **Humor Appeal**

Humor is an element that is used in around 30% of the advertisements. Humor can be an excellent tool to catch the viewer's attention and help in achieving instant recall which can work well for the sale of the product. Humor can be used effectively when it is related to some benefit that the customer can derive without which the joke might overpower the message.

- **Sex Appeal**

Sex and nudity have always sold well. Sexuality, sexual suggestiveness, over sexuality or sensuality raises curiosity of the audience and can result in strong feelings about the advertisement. It can also result in the product appearing interesting. However use of sex in types of advertising appeals can have a boomerang effect if it is not used carefully. It can interfere with the actual message of the advertisement and purpose of the product and can also cause low brand recall. If this is used then it should be an integral part of the product and should not seem vulgar. The shift should be towards sensuality.

- **Music Appeal**

Music can be used as types of advertising appeals as it has a certain intrinsic value and can help in increasing the persuasiveness of the advertisement. It can also help capture attention and increase customer recall.

- **Scarcity Appeal**

Scarcity appeals are based on limited supplies or limited time period for purchase of products and are often used while employing promotional tools including sweepstakes, contests etc.

- **Rational Appeal**

Rational appeals as the name suggests aims to focus on the individual's functional, utilitarian or practical needs for particular products and services. Such appeals emphasize the characteristics and features of the product and the service and how it would be beneficial to own or use the particular brand. Print media is particularly well suited for rational appeals and is often used with good success. It is also suited for business to business advertisers and for products that are complex and that need high degree of attention and involvement.

- **Masculine / Feminine Appeal**

Used in cosmetic or beauty products and also clothing. This type of appeal aims at creating the impression of the perfect person. The message is that the product will infuse the perfection or the stated qualities in you. E.g. *Real men wear Wrangler Jeans! Or "Stag, a man's beer!"*

- **Brand Appeal**

This appeal is directed towards people who are brand conscious and wish to choose particular products to make a brand statement.

- **Snob Appeal**

This appeal is directed towards creating feeling of desire or envy for products that are termed top of the line or that have considerable qualities of luxury, elegance associated with them. E.g. *Why drive a Honda, when there is a Lexus?*

- **Adventure Appeal**

This appeal is directed towards giving the impression that purchasing a product will change the individual's life radically and fill it with fun, adventure and action. E.g. *Disney Family fun Adventure*

- **Less than Perfect Appeal**

Advertisements often try to influence people to make certain purchases by pointing out their inadequacies or making them feel less perfect and more dissatisfied with their present condition. These types of advertising appeals are used in cosmetic and health industries.

- **Romance Appeal**

These advertisements display the attraction between the sexes. The appeal is used to signify that buying certain products will have a positive impact on the opposite sex and improve your romantic or love life. Perfumes, cars and other products use these types of advertising appeals.

- **Emotional Words/Sensitivity Appeal**

These advertisements are used to drive at and influence the sensitivities of consumers.

- **Youth Appeal**

Advertisements that reflect youth giving aspects or ingredients of products use these types of appeals. Cosmetic products in particular make use of these appeals. E.g. *Olay Regenerist guaranteed to give you younger skin*

- **Endorsement**

Celebrities and well known personalities often endorse certain products and their pitching can help drive the sales. E.g. *Melanie Hudson advertising for Weight Loss.*

- **Play on Words**

Advertisements also make effective use of catch phrases to convey the message. Such appeals help in brand recognition and recall and can be quite popular with the youth in particular. E.g. *Image is Nothing! Thirst is Everything! Obey your thirst!*

- **Statistics**

Advertisements also use statistics and figures to display aspects of the product and its popularity in particular.

- **Plain Appeal**

These advertisements use every day aspects of life and appeal to ordinary people regarding the use of a product or service. E.g. *It's so easy to use Geico.com, even a Caveman can use it!*

- **Bandwagon Appeal**

This type of advertising appeal is meant to signify that since everybody is doing something you should be a part of the crowd as well. It appeals towards the popularity aspect or coolness aspect of a person using a particular product or service.

115. **Campaigns**

What is a Campaign Strategy?

A campaign can be seen as an organized, purposeful effort to create change, and it should be guided by thoughtful planning. Before taking action, successful campaigners learn as much as possible about:

- The existing situation; what problem are you confronting?
- Who is affected by the campaign issue both positively and negatively? Who are the stakeholders? Who are you trying to reach?
- How are these people or groups related to the problem and to each other
- What changes could improve the situation
- What resources, strategies and audio visuals aids/tools are available to implement a campaign that will address the issue?

Campaigners then use this knowledge to create their strategy, which guides them in planning, implementing, marketing, monitoring, improving and evaluating their campaign.

Use words, diagrams and illustrations that are relevant to your campaign.

It's useful to involve your whole campaigning group in exploring the *problem*, your *vision* and the *changes* sought: a shared understanding of the problem will stimulate ideas about possible actions to take, and will also help your group to stay motivated and focused during the campaign. Creating a common vision will also help determine ways to monitor, and adjust the implementation of, the campaign if necessary.

Understand the Campaign's Stakeholders

Stakeholders are people, groups, organizations, or institutions that are connected to your issue. They may support your campaign, be adversely affected by the issue in question, have the power to change the situation, or even be responsible for the problem you have identified. An important task when designing your campaign is to learn as much about the stakeholders as possible. You should:

- Understand each stakeholder's relationship to the problem and your proposed solution
- Define the relationships between different stakeholders
- Determine the ability and potential of stakeholders to help or hurt your campaign
- Identify which of these stakeholders your campaign should concentrate on to create the change you desire.

116. Proposals

Basically, a **proposal** is a document that is created with the sole intention of persuading the reader(s). In your proposal there are three elements that you aim at addressing:

- There is a significant problem
- You have a solution

- You are the person who should create the solution

A proposal is a persuasive / argumentative document in which you address the three situations mentioned above.

As usual, in a proposal as with your speech and advertisement, you need to consider your audience, your readers, when you persuade. Some readers will be persuaded by one idea or type of argument, but that same idea or argument might not have any effect at all on another reader.

When you argue, again you need to use four basic strategies:

- *Logic* or *logos* where you present facts and logical connections
- *Emotions or ethos* where you appeal to your audience on an emotional level
- *Character* where you show in your proposal that you or your team are good, trustworthy and suitable to do the job
- *Ethics or ethos* where you show that you propose to do what you put forward because it is the moral or ethical thing to do

117. **Speaking**

It is wise to think before you speak. There are four preliminary questions you should ask yourself before you open your mouth:

- *Do I have anything to say?*
- *What message do I want to give?*
- *What is the level of information of the listeners?*
- *How much time do I have to give my message?*

The first question is quite important. In a particular situation you may not have anything to say for a variety of reasons. If this is so then you do not speak. Sometimes it is wise to be silent. The fact that you have two ears but one mouth, suggests that you should listen twice as much as you speak.

Most times you have something to say, but you have so much information on the particular point in issue, you must ask yourself—what message do I want to convey? When you establish the message you want to give, or the point you want to make, then your speaking can be focused.

The level of information the listeners have about the matter you are going to speak about must be considered. For example, if you were speaking to someone about the splendor of last carnival, you will speak differently depending on whether you were speaking to a visitor who never saw carnival, as opposed to someone who had seen five previous carnivals but missed the last one.

The time in which you have to give your message will also dictate how you express yourself. If you only had one minute to make your point, your communication will be different to if you had 30 minutes, and still different if you had two hours. An example may make this point clearer. If you were asked to talk about your achievements in life, and you were given 5 minutes to tell your story, it will be differently presented than if you had been given one hour in which to do it.

118. Contexts of communication

Communication does not take place in a vacuum. Between communicators, the process takes place in a particular communication situation where the identifiable elements of the process work in a dynamic interrelation. This situation is referred to as the *context*—the when and where of a communication event. Communication contexts vary depending on the need, purpose, number of communicators and the ways exchange is taking place. Communication can be conducted in an intrapersonal, interpersonal, small group, organizational, academic, cultural or inter-cultural and public context or situation. Knowing the elements of communication will lead to a more meaningful understanding of the processes. You communicate and you know it is important for you. To communicate effectively, you need to have an understanding of how these elements work together in a process.

When you communicate within yourself, it is called **intrapersonal** communication. This is interplay within yourself through asking and answering questions that you pose to yourself. In a sense, it is monologue. Writing notes to help you remember is one example of intrapersonal context of communication.

Communicating with one other person is called **interpersonal** communication. In this context, the burden of communicating is high. You either get your message across, or you fail 100% to get your message across to the other person. The need for clarity and effectiveness is critical.

When you are communicating to a **small group,** you have a good chance to know your audience and to pitch your message effectively. This is especially so, if it is a homogeneous group with a common understanding of the intended message. A group of scientists, businessmen, stock brokers, or educators would be cases in point.

In the **organizational context** information goes up and down hierarchies such as the CEO, through to the high level managers to the low level managers, the supervisors then to the workers. Communication in an **intercultural context** takes place when persons of different cultures communicate with each other through the various mediums of communication. Intercultural communication may also occur across sub-groups within the same society for example in our Caribbean context there exist many cultures within any one island and as such intercultural communication takes place amongst the various cultural groups. A simple example of intercultural context of communication can be observed in the process of tour guiding.

Writing essays, research papers, theses and dissertations are all examples of communication in the **academic context.**

Communication to a **public** or **mass audience** is challenging, but it can be done effectively. A mass audience would comprise of persons with differing levels of knowledge and consciousness of the message being communicated. Perhaps 10% of the audience would not understand what you are saying. Another 10% will find that your content is too basic, and not deep enough. It is the remaining 80% that you have to shift with your message. This underscores the importance of knowing your audience. You have to know your audience to determine what to say and how to say it. This is especially so with a live audience with which you have live contact.

You may have a **mass** audience through radio, television, podcast, cable, or MP 3 streaming. In this case, you may not be able to know who your audience really is. It will take a lot of research and imagination to analyze that audience. In such a case, a good rule is to keep the material clear and simple. The 80% of such mass audiences tend to be not too sophisticated.

CONTEXTS OF COMMUNICATION

Intrapersonal	**Communicating with self**
Interpersonal	**Communicating with another person**
Small group	**Communicating with less than 10 persons together**
Organizational	**Communicating in a business context or situation**
Academic	**Communicating in an educational context or situation**
Public/mass	**Communicating to the public**
Intercultural	**Communicating across social sub-groups**

119. Exposition or Oral Presentation Skills

Your oral presentation is an integral part of your Portfolio (**16 marks**) and as such you need to make an effective presentation to your teacher if you are to gain top marks. Delivering a clearly understandable message requires that you put in as much practice as you can. Remember that whilst you are allowed to have one cue card in your presentation—**<u>you are not allowed to consistently read from it.</u>**

Experts tell us that public speaking or oral presentation ranks highest on the list of situations that people fear the most, followed by death. Overcoming this dread requires **proper preparation and persistent practice, practice, practice.**

120. Tips for improving your presentation skills

- Know your topic as this is very important
- Prepare for your oral presentation. Deliver your topic to your friends, family and to yourself. Even professional speakers take time to prepare and practice their delivery.
- Ask your friends and family for feedback
- Prepare as you take your cue card with your main points it will help you to trigger your thoughts
- On the day of your presentation be relaxed and confident.
- Remember the importance of non verbal cues

121. Study Tips for Success

- Set the goal to succeed in this exam!
- Communication Studies is one of the easiest subjects at CAPE level but as with most subjects that you know is easy, you take them for granted and you do not study for it. The end result is that you fail to get the best result in your exams!
- The first step to succeeding in CAPE is discipline. The definition of discipline that I accept is "Doing what needs to be done, when it needs to be done, EVEN when I don't want to or feel like doing it!
- Discipline does not only get you doing what you have to do but it covers your tendency to procrastinate and to mis-manage your time. Be discipline and you are ready for success!
- With my students I begin with Module 1, then Module 3 and end with Module 2.

- When studying Paper 1A always read ALL parts to the question first. Some students forget this and write answers without reading all the parts only to realize most times that they gave the wrong answer in the earlier part. This is time wasting and sometimes costs you a mark.
- Use your Past Papers to practice doing as many as you can.
- The student who is able to easily discuss the various concepts of Communication is the student who is most likely to succeed at this subject. Find classmates and discuss the subject!

122. Conclusion

The manner and form in which people use to communicate differs dramatically. The older society was more accustomed to using speech rather than text to communicate. They were greeted with smiles. They engaged in active listening and devoted their full attention to the person with whom they were communicating. They ended with a warm goodbye. Now, people can answer messages whenever they feel like they have the time to do it. Conversations can be ended just as randomly and quickly as they started. Feelings and moods are conveyed by their choice of words or symbols for "Emoticons." On the other hand, people in the past easily expressed their emotions with non-verbal communication.

Communication is often recognized as the foundation of any society. It seems very difficult to even begin to perceive life without it. The major aim of the subject, *Communication Studies,* is to make you consciously competent in such skills as research, writing, listening, presenting, using technology and speaking.

Communication Studies also seeks to expose you to greater opportunities to enhance and master your use of the standard language of your country. Your mastery at the language level will allow you to understand the interconnectivity between language itself and your social and cultural identities.

Communication Studies will be behind the times if it were not geared to discussing the impact of technology on all levels and acts of communication.

As hectic as your school schedule may be now think about how much more hectic it will be later on, whether you choose to further your studies or to enter the world of work. Making good decisions that will impact on your future require careful research, planning and analysis—all of which you are exposed to in *Communication Studies.*

EXHIBITS

Exhibit "A" Listening Comprehension exercise with answers

Vagrants! Vagrants! Vagrants! The city is swarming with vagrants-vagrants in the street, vagrants on the pavement, vagrants sleeping under store fronts and vagrants digging and turning over bins and boxes! Vagrants mixing and mingling with decent, busy people hustling to get to work! Our country is now reduced to vagrancy!

What are our honorable parliamentarians doing about this most disgusting situation?

Has anything been done except talk, talk, and more talk?

And after all is said and done—nothing is done!

Do they really think that they can fool us? Don't they realize that we are fed-up of the way they take us for granted?

Perhaps I can recount a recent incident that showed me clearly how unreliable, slow to act and how concerned about human suffering the service institutions in our country are. I was almost shocked to death at the lightning speed with which they were able to pass the responsibility on to another agency.

I came upon a female vagrant lying in apparent agony on the pavement. She had been severely beaten and left for dead. She needed medical attention. I called the police who quickly referred me to the Fire Service who in turn promptly passed me to the Health Department who apologetically referred me to the Casualty Department of the Port of Spain General Hospital who personnel lived up to the name! Well, thanks to these humane and casually considerate institutions for their prompt efficiency.

A dead vagrant arrived at the hospital having kicked the bucket on the pavement. You cannot imagine how pleased I was to see a vagrant die because of a vagrant government. I thought to myself "so shall you live so shall you die" So much for our caring government and public services.

QUESTIONS

1. *In a sentence of no more than 20 words, state the main idea of the passage.*
2. *Identify 2 literary devices used in the extract and give one example of each*
3. *Comment on the effectiveness of each device identified above*
4. *What is the tone of the extract? Give two examples to support your answer.*

ANSWERS

1. *The main idea of the extract is the inefficiency (or apparent inefficiency) of our major institutions in times of an emergency.*
2. *Literary devices used in the extract are: Rhetorical questions, repetition, exaggeration/hyperbole, personal anecdotes, sarcasm*

   Examples of devices: **rhetorical questions** *"Do they really think that they can fool us?"*

   Repetition: *"Vagrants! Vagrants! Vagrants!"*

   Hyperbole *"almost shocked to death" ". . . The lightning speed with which they performed their duties."*

   Personal anecdotes *"Perhaps I can recount a recent incident that showed me . . ."*

   Sarcasm *"you cannot imagine how pleased I was to see a vagrant die . . ." and "well, thanks to these humane and considerate institutions for their prompt efficiency . . ."*
3. **Rhetorical questions** *call reader to question/think about the issue at hand in this case the issue of the slow inefficient pace at which service institutions operate.*

3b. Exaggeration *helps the author to achieve his purpose showing the lack of alacrity of the workers in these institutions.*

4. *The* **tone** *of the extract was one of sarcasm or condemnation or criticism or one of complaint.*

4b. **Example "...** *how pleased I was to see a vagrant die because of a vagrant government.*

4c. "Well thanks to these humane and considerate institutions for their prompt efficiency . . ."

Exhibit "B" sample essay for module one

Question taken from Past Papers 2003-2007

The writer's main point is that tourists are drawn to St John because of its natural, pristine unspoiled beauty.

Pam Carlson in her article puts forth strong points in her desire to persuade her readers and potential visitors that indeed St John is the ideal tourist vacation site. To achieve this she employs many strategies and language techniques which have made this an effective piece.

Firstly she employs literary devices and strategies such as similes, metaphors, personification, hyperbole, compare and contrast, emotive language and historical data. The emotive language such as "kissed", "welcomed me" and "caressed" appealed to our senses in an attempt to evoke from the readers feelings of deep appreciation for the island of St John. The literary device of personification can be seen in the sentence "Trade winds kissed me as I stepped off the airplane in St Thomas. Like playful sprites they tugged my hair and caressed my skin". The use of this device helps the writer achieve her purpose of luring tourists to the island that she believes to be a beautiful place.

In the second paragraph the writer used the strategy of comparison and contrast as she emphasized that "there are no mainstream tourist attractions" in her effort to show the uniqueness of the island. An additional strategy is her use of the simile as seen in the words "this is an island where beautiful beaches are strung out like pearls on a chain . . ." This device made the island appear even more intriguing and exotic to the reader tempting any tourist.

Historical facts or data are used when she wrote "Caneal Bay was founded by Laurence Rockefeller, who stumbled on the island during a 1920's sailing trip. This historical fact serve to strengthen her case for getting tourists to visit the island as it adds credibility to the information that she has presented.

Her use of exaggeration as a strategy is meant to peak the reader's interest in visiting St John. The words such as "manicured", "idyllic", and "unspoiled" highlight the beauty of the island and help the writer to achieve her purpose.

The techniques and strategies employed by the author Pam Carlson are all very effective as they all worked together in achieving the purpose of getting tourists to choose St John as their ideal vacation sight.

(385 words)

Exhibit "C" second sample of Module One essay

Essay question taken from Past Papers 2011

The writer's main point in this extract was the immense destructive power of tsunamis and the detrimental effects that they can have on an area. His purpose aims at creating awareness in his readers of the catastrophic ability of these waves to cause destruction and also to educate them about the factors affecting the formation of these gigantic waves. He accomplishes this through the use of various organizational strategies and language techniques.

One such strategy which the author employed extensively was the provision of facts and statistics or figures. For example, he lets his readers know the average speed of a tsunami when travelling in open water and also some of the factors which can affect the ways in which a tsunami is formed such as slope and shape of the sea floor. By doing this the author proves to the readers that he is not only well educated on the topic but that he is achieving his purpose of warning them of the tsunami's power and potential to destroy everything and everyone in its path.

Additionally, the writer utilizes the strategy of comparison as he describes the tsunamis to ocean waves telling us that it was "*like referring to firecrackers and atomic warheads both as explosives*" and also when he described the speed of a tsunami to the speed of a jetliner. This is a very appropriate strategy as it gives the reader a better understanding of how powerful and destructively fast tsunamis are.

The recalling of past events was another strategy that the writer used to achieve his purpose. The writer chose to refer to two deadly tsunamis that struck Chile in 1960 and Japan in 1993 leaving destruction in its path. In recalling these tsunami occurrences the writer also presented first hand or eyewitness accounts of survivors of both experiences. The writer does this to probably instill a sense of the fear that a tsunami attack can evoke in people as they see the "*dark wall of water*" approaching.

Together with organizational strategies the writer used language techniques to ensure that his purpose is achieved. For example his use of both visual and auditory metaphor to describe tsunamis as "*dark walls" and "waves bulldozing into the shore*" allow readers to visualize the destructive and immense power of the tsunamis.

Including emotive words that invoke both visual and auditory images in the mind of the reader is an effective language technique that also allows the writer to achieve his purpose. Examples such as "*attack*", "*overwhelm*", '*snapping trees like twigs*" "*smashing houses*" effectively serve to help the writer achieve his purpose of showing the great power of a tsunami.

The final language technique that the writer used was that of a mixing the elements of narrative and exposition which only serve to heighten the readers sense of the imminent danger and destructive power of tsunamis.

Through the writer's use of various organizational strategies and techniques he was able to put forward his main point and achieve his purpose at the same time. His readers were able to have a clear description of the destructive power and speed of tsunamis from reading this adaptation by Daniel Pendick.

Exhibit "D" two sample essays for paper 02 module two

Essay question from Past Papers 2003-2007
TALK DAT TALK

In this excerpt one can see that the writer employed both the creole and the Standard English. It can also be seen that people's perception of the use of either of these languages differs in many ways. To many persons, the use of the creole language is looked down on and is thought of as "backward" while Standard English is perceived to be the finest language.

Taffy appears to have a fair command of the English language and his possible motivation for achieving this command of English is to appear intelligent. Taffy believes that the creole language is "backward and foolish"; he believes that by using this "perfect English" he would be able to progress in his everyday life. Taffy describes the creole language as having "funny words" seemingly seeing creole as ideally a language for comic relief. Taffy does not want to be classed with the others in his village and he says "There is no place for your backward Trini dialect." The villagers on the other hand seem to strongly disagree with Taffy over his preference of Standard English. Both Olga and Boysie openly defended the creole with passion and pride. They were highly offended when Taffy described the creole language as being "backward and foolish."

Olga's passion for creole is very pronounced as she defends her belief saying that "Trini talk is not bad English is jus' a special way." She also believes that people can code-switch whenever and wherever they feel they deem necessary as we are quite capable of moving from creole to standard English with ease as she says "Trinis know when and where to speak the standard English." For Boysie talking Trini creole identifies us as nothing but Trinidadian . . . "de way we talk give we Trinis an identity." Olga and Boysie appear to be proud to use the creole.

It is well known that a video presentation will greatly enhance this language situation in that it allows for the audience to see the non-verbal communications which took place, mainly the characters body language, gestures and facial expressions. For example the viewing audience will be able to see the shock on both Boysie and Olga's face when Taffy walked in to Mr. Chin village shop and asked for "crackers and candy." It also allows the reader to see the proxemics in the way the characters used space and their vocalics.

In conclusion, it can be seen in this excerpt that people's attitudes to language fuel their motivation and choice of language. Making a language choice should be someone's prerogative but in many cases the choice comes with negative against the language that is not chosen. In this excerpt we see Boysie and Olga exhibiting pride and confidence as they defended their choice of creole. Taffy like many persons made the choice of Standard English because he believed that it will help him in many areas of his life.

(484 words)

ESSAY 2

TALK DAT TALK

Creole usually refers to languages that result from contact between the language of the colonizing peoples and the language of the colonized people. Caribbean society, in general assigns high value to standard language as opposed to Creole. However, some individuals choose to take pride in their Creole language and view it as an identity marker. The excerpt "*Talk dat Talk*!" is a perfect example of this.

In the passage, it is evident that the man called Taffy places great importance on achieving a good command of the English language. One of Taffy's motivations fro achieving a good command of the English language seems to be so that he can be understood abroad by foreigners. In the passage he said that if he continued to speak the Creole language, people in New York would not understand him. He also seems to respect and value the Standard English and associates prestige with its use whereas he refers to the Creole as having "funny words."

Another reason for his motivation is that he believes that a good command of the English will help him achieve success and upward mobility. He even purchased books that he believes will teach his daughters how to "progress and do well" and speak "de proper way" this shows that he believes that the standard English is proper as opposed to the Creole that is improper. To him the reason why he has not chosen to embrace Creole is that it is "backward."

Choice of language is personal and for Boysie and Olga the Creole was their main choice of language. In the passage they defended it vociferously revealing their pride in their Trini language. Olga responded to Taffy's denigration of the Creole by telling him that Creole should be something to inspire pride because it is a historical and cultural legacy from our African, Amerindian and Indian ancestors. Boysie supported this by adding that Creole was indeed a language just like Standard English retorting that if Taffy believed that Creole had "funny words" then Standard English had even stranger words and even breaks the rules of its own language! To them both Creole was what identified them as true Trinis.

This is a dramatic passage and a video presentation would greatly enhance the written words. Aspects of non-verbal communication, that is, kinesics and vocalic would be enhanced. The paralangue such as tone of voice, volume, pitch and rate of the characters input would be emphasized. It would be great to see Taffy's shame and embarrassment as he lost the argument.

A video presentation will certainly enhance this poem as it would act as a visual stimulus particularly to the setting of the shop and the way in which the characters presented themselves.

The attitudes formulated to language give persons a preconceived judgment of other people and their language choice. As seen in this poem there were conflicting beliefs and motivations. Whilst Taffy argued vehemently in favor of his choice of the Standard English Olga and Boysie argued in favor of their choice, the Creole.

(506 words)

Exhibit "E" sample answer for paper 02 section C

May/June 2003. Module 3 Essay

Good afternoon ladies and gentlemen of Sunville, I am Richard Lewis, the head of the environment protection group known as The Environment Inspectors. My purpose this afternoon is to inform you of the large shipments of nuclear waste that is being transported through our waters as well as the harmful consequences which it may have on our community if this problem persists. My group is preparing for a protest march against this problem and we would like all of you to come out in your numbers and make a choice, let your voices be heard. Come make a choice!

A community meeting would be held on a Sunday afternoon at 5 pm at the local community center. This time and location was chosen as persons are usually home at this time and have usually finished all their chores. The location is also convenient to all members of the community. This method chosen is appropriate as the community members would be able to interact and voice their concerns and ideas on the matter. Speech would be chosen as the medium as the speaker would be able to relate to the audience and clarify any questions.

As the head of the group, I am determined to protect our beautiful community from these harsh consequences which would result if this illegal act continues. Do you remember ten years ago in 1989 when Venezuela suffered? Tens of thousands of the fishes died as a result of this nuclear waste. Their oceans were polluted and citizens were falling ill. Do you remember that day when the breaking news reported that fifty children died after being exposed to the pollution? Women were giving birth to handicapped children. Do you remember? Do you want this to happen to you and your children? (raise voice) Make a choice!! Come out in your numbers and let your voices be heard. Allow our community of Sunville to be bright once again; where your children can play free from diseases, mothers can give birth to healthy babies. Make a choice! Put a stop to this illegal activity that is taking over our precious waters. Make a choice! Think about you children, your nieces, nephews, grand-children. Make a choice! Give them a clean non-polluted life. I leave it in your hands now to come out and Make a choice!!!!

Exhibit "F" Commentary

The composition is appropriate as it allows the community members to see the emotion in the speaker through his tone, pitch and rate of his voice. It allows immediate feedback and the speaker is able to read non-verbal communication from the community members. It is also appropriate as it exposes the community members to the consequences that they may face if they do not make a choice. The use of the tag line '*Make a choice*!' also alerts the people that it is their decision to put a stop to the illegal activity and it gives them a sense of responsibility to their children, therefore they may react faster. The reality that their children may as a result of this situation may also make them aware of the harsh consequences that they may face. All these can be push factors for them to join the protest and *Make a Choice*!

Exhibit "G" sample portfolio

"Fashion: Its Influence On Female Teenagers"

General Introduction

The Merriam-Webster Dictionary describes fashion as '*the prevailing style (as in dress) during a particular time"* and this forms the theme of my Communication Studies portfolio **"Fashion: Its Influence on Female Teenagers."**

In the expository which is the first of three sections I presented a seven minute speech to my teacher in which I shared on topics such as the history of our local fashion industry, the importance of and link between teenagers and fashion. In this section I also collected and used as secondary sources two articles on the same topic. For my reflective section, I chose to show in monologue genre titled, *"Confessions of a Fashion Crazed Teen"* how deeply fashion can influence teenagers. This monologue is accompanied by a rationale that gives an account of my inspiration, purpose, intended audience and the context in which this piece may be used. I have chosen to analyze the monologue in terms of registers and communicative behaviors found therein.

I am seriously interested in this theme because I truly want to know everything that deals with teenage fashion so that my friends and I can keep up to date with the trends. Academically I have realized that knowledge of fashion helps me to keep up with certain areas in my Clothing and Textiles classes. As a future Fashion Journalist it is imperative that I am always in the know about what happening in the fashion industry.

Expository
Fashion: Its Influence on Female Teenagers

Introduction:

Good Morning Mrs Rochford. I am here to present my theme "Fashion: Its Influence on Female Teenagers. I begin with a quote from English writer Quentin Crisp and I quote, "Fashion is what you adopt when you don't know who you are."
Is this an appropriate definition of fashion? Some will agree, some will disagree but I will play is safe and say that it is partly true and false because of where you focussing.

Fashion and the fashion industry is an ever-present force in our society and continue to evolve and gain strength day by day.

Fashion can be described as exciting, ever changing, a form of personal expression or even a display of self-concept. The question remains though: is the industry gaining strength or gathering more minions?

There is no doubt of the influence fashion has on female teens around the world. From the obvious way they dress, to the attitudes and behaviours that are adopted and the creation of social statues. Just look at teen personalities as Miley Cyrus and Justin Bieber and see how young people nearly literally clone themselves to be like them.

So who influences the fashion choices of these females? Who determines trends? Is there really a link between fashion choices and social status? Does fashion ever become a problem? These issues and more will be explored in this expository as we tackle 'Female Teenagers and Fashion'.

Background

The focus of my expository is our local fashion industry, which only in recent times has begun to gather momentum. Many persons believe that Trinidad fashion is possibly the most important thing in Trinidad next to Trinidad Carnival. The clothes and fashion designs are as diverse as the ethnicities, races and cultures that take residence here.
The development of the industry locally is long in coming, but progress can been seen with the popular Trinidad and Tobago Fashion Week (TTFW) going into its fourth year, fashion Degrees are now being offered at The University Of Trinidad and Tobago (UTT) and the formation of The Fashion Association of Trinidad and Tobago (FATT) in September 2010 to promote the industry are but just some of the ideas that are mushrooming and building our fashion industry.

Local fashion editor, Marcus Marin (pseudonym) my primary source, whom I had the pleasure of interviewing, describes local fashion as "*Evolving*" because "*What it is now, it wasn't a while ago*". He notices now that "*The general public is suddenly fashion conscious*" with fashion in Trinidad and Tobago finally becoming a "*Breathable entity*".

While the local industry is still making baby steps, the influence from and on an international level still remains.

Fashion and female teenagers

Females in their teenage years are at a point of self-discovery and often use fashion to communicate to the world what their personality really says. Marcus says that female teens use fashion as a form of "*self-expression*". But is it self-expression or the product of a manipulative and provocative industry? While at the end of the day, it comes down to personal choice and preferences; the industry still has its pull.

Who influences fashion choices and trends among teenaged females?

Television shows, movies, the Internet, music videos and especially fashion magazines; these media are all part of the social environment in which today's young people grow up and they can contribute to setting social norms. Collectively, they are known as 'mass media'. They are where the influence begins on these ladies.

They portray images and ideas that tell us teens what is good for us and thus enticing us to follow them. These are the effects of mass media in teenagers; teenagers buy what they see on TV, what their favourite celebrity advertises and what is acceptable by society based on the fashion that the media has imposed on them.

Link between fashion choices and social status

I have found out that there is a definite link between the fashion choices of female teenagers and their perceptions of social status. Whether a teenaged female want it or not she seems unable to avoid being influenced in some way by whatever is trending in the fashion world. For most teenagers their persona is highlighted through their sense of fashion. For example on our School Bazaar Day one can see the girls who are influence by the Gothic look or the Hollywood look.

Fashion is a social statement. It is an outward means of expression. Thus, a teen's fashion choice denotes her social status. Asked whether there is a link between fashion choices and social status, Marcus answered "*Indeed, fashion provides teenagers a sense of identity by signaling which 'grouping' they belong to.*

Based on fashion choices, teen females can be classed as '*prep*', '*punk*', '*goth*', or '*emo*' among numerous other groupings. It may also signal a more independent or inclusive personality. Fashion and the lack thereof can communicate whether the female is a member of high, middle or low class society, each with its attached stereotyping. This self-expression can also lead to judgment and bullying from her peers as well.

Appropriateness of fashion

Fashion choices made by teen females may be a means of identity and self-expression, but are these choices always appropriate?

Often fashions that appear on the runways are over-the-top and inappropriate for teenage wear. If teenagers see these fashion trends, they may be tempted to try them.
In an effort to keep up with current trends fed to her by mass media, a young girl may lose herself and become another 'mannequin' of fashion, donning each and everything that she considered 'fashionable'. What is considered fashionable may not always be appropriate to situations a teen may find herself in or her age. For example, mini skirts may be the trend, but boundaries are crossed when a girl wears one to church or formal gathering 'for the sake of fashion'. Thus, fashion choices need be tailored to the context.

The choice may also be appropriate to cultural norms, for example, Muslims wear hijabs due to the requirements of their religion.

When does fashion become a problem?

There comes a point however, at which fashion may be considered problematic. I believe that when it is used as a tool of peer pressure or rebellion. For example in this school it is mandatory that we wear our full uniform to school but, a rebellious student many just decide that that is too restrictive an come to school dressed in casual clothes.
Young girls are at a stage in their life where they want to be accepted by their peers, they want to be loved and be successful and most times will do almost anything to achieve this. Fashion is for most of them the only way to show of the person they think they are. The

fashion industry creates the ideal image of a beautiful woman; you can see it in fashion magazines, movies and on television. The subliminal messages tell young females that, "*If you are not like them you are not cool, so you should buy the stuff they buy and look like they do.*"

Many teens pick up on fashion trends in an effort to stave off humiliation and mocking from peers. Poor fashion choices in the eyes of others can often be an open door to ridicule.

Rebellion may also be acted out via fashion. Since rebellion is often a huge aspect of a teenager's life, it is not shocking that teens often use licentious or shocking fashion to rebel against their parents, their classmates, and/or society. For example the shorter, the tighter, the more exposed flesh the better to rebel against parents, school and society on the whole.

Conclusion

Fashion is what's current and what is '*in the moment*'. It often evokes interest in a large number of people, especially teenaged females. The clothes we wear tell a lot about ourselves and furthermore, our social standings. Fashion is so important to girls because it is a way to self express in a world that seems to be constantly telling them what they can and cannot do. It has evolved throughout the years along with society. Teenagers are influenced by mass media and their choices are not always appropriate. It has become a way of life for some and they are often are consumed by fashion, leading to peer pressure and rebellion.

All in all, the fashion industry and the obvious influence it has on female teens, comes down to a matter of personal choice and preference.

Challenges experience in exploring selected topic

In my research for information and articles on my selected topic: "Fashion: Its Influence on Female Teenagers" my major obstacle was time management. My week is filled with a variety of activities and responsibilities and as such creating time to do research was often a problem. Another challenge was the frequent mal-functioning of my home Wifi so I couldn't get onto the Internet.

Evaluation of the effect of source, context and medium on the reliability and validity of information gathered

The information gathered in the putting together of this expository was collected over the World Wide Web. Additional information was also attained through an interview I conducted with local Fashion Editor, Marcus Marin. I must also add that information was also included through my personal knowledge and experience with fashion.

While the Internet may not always be the most reliable resource, I consider the information I collected through it very reliable and valid for this particular topic, as fashion is all over the Internet.

Marcus is very experienced in his field, having been exposed and part of fashion on a local and international level, so the information I collected through his interview I consider very reliable and valid.

My personal additions to my expository, I consider reliable and valid as well as I have personal experience in the fashion industry on a local level. Being a teenage female and having experienced a lot of what is contained in this expository further add to reliability and validity of the information I presented.
I end with a quote by Lord Chesterfield, a British statesman and diplomat:

"If you are not in fashion, you are nobody."

Additional articles for expository

http://michaelkorswatcheswomen.com/media-influences-our-fashion-choices/

http://www.ehow.com/how-does_5542625_do-magazines-affect-teen-fashion.html

Preface

For my reflective I have composed a monologue entitled "*Confessions of a Fashion Crazed Teen*".

I have chosen this genre because I believe that it is most appropriate medium in which Katherina can self express her absolute love for fashion and how it influences her every action.

The purpose of the piece is to further emphasize and show the influence of fashion on female teens, through the persona of Katherina. Although slightly comical, it is meant to highlight effects of this influence on teens.

My intended audience is firstly, teenaged females like myself, aged 16-19 years and secondly, the young and upcoming members of the fashion community including designers, editors and models.

The piece would be best presented either as an opening item or during the intermission at a fashion show to provide entertainment and food for thought. It can also be presented during an ethics class to initiate discussion on the various factors that influence female teenagers.

Reflective

Confessions of a Fashion Crazed Teen

Hi.
My name is Katherina, yes Katherina Marguerite Ebony LaSalle.
I'm 17 and I'm told I have a problem.
They say I'm "*Obsessed with fashion*", I mean I don't think I'm '*obsessed*' I just love to be wearing the latest Louis Vuitton.
And Chanel,
And Gucci,
And Versace,
And Prada . . . muahhhh
And rock the newest Christian LeBoutine's, Steven Madden is a must!
Ok so maybe I am just a little bit obsessed.
It's not my fault I NEEEEEEED to be in the trendiest clothes, I have an image to uphold!
Look when I am in my best I'm constantly complimented:
{Dialectal variation} "*Kat, I love those shoes, where'd you get dem?*" with looks of awe.
That question never gets old. Next time I think I'll say "*No where you can get them.*"
Smiling from ear to ear.
I mean, I have to be exclusive, we fashionistas can't reveal our sources!
"*Oh my, you look fabulous Kathy!*"
The pride written all over my face is the only response I give them.
Hands down, there's no other girl in my lane.
I laugh when I see a fake brand; I mean have some class ladies.
If you can't afford it, don't wear it!
You might say I'm spoilt, but I just talk the truth.
Imagine one time Mother bought ME a Caribbean Belle magazine.
Haha . . . I had such a good laugh.
Caribbean fashion? Daz is local fashion? Eh eh not for me? {**Dialectal variation**}

HA! Not for moi . . . Ms Katherina Marguerite Ebony LaSalle!
Mother HAS got to buy me the absolute latest Vogue, Elle, Glamour and In Style Magazines. **{Dialectal variation}**
{Communicative behaviour} I'm only interested in American and European trends thank you!
I just HAVE to visit New York, L.A., Paris or Milan at least twice a year to shop, if I don't . . . I feel so incomplete.
Those trips are always the best!
This one time . . . I remember spotting this gorgeous Fendi handbag in NY back in summer of '10.
Of course I had to have it.
As I laid hands on it, so did another lady who was eyeing it as well. Although I hate speaking that way, I knew that this was no time for fancy English; it was time to speak my mind in a way that that woman would have understand . . . and besides . . . the bag had my name on it!
{Dialectal variation} *"Leh go of mih darn bag! Is mine! It ha mih name on it! An besides I see it fuss"* perspiring a bit now.
{Attitude to language}The lady stared back at me. You should see: her mouth wide open like a fish 'haha' and eyebrows up to her forehead like arrows. **{Communicative behaviours}** If the situation were not so serious I would have laughed.
I had to do what I had to!
The manager came over
{Dialectal variation and Register} *"Oh, good day Sir, sorry for the disturbance, but I must have this bag."*
Her face was dumbstruck once again.
Soon after offering twice the price, the bag was mine.
Wouldn't you have done the same?
I have only one close friend. Her name is Leanne.
It's so hard to make the cut to roll with someone like me
But Leanne is so much like me, such a fashionista!
Although she can never do it like I do
(Shhh! don't tell her I said that)
{Register} *"Right this way Ms. La Salle"* as we skip in front the line at the clubs
. . . leaving those other females to eat my Jimmy Choo dust!
*"Who iz dat!"****{Dialectal variation}***

I often hear the guys say as I pass batting my eyelashes checking my face in my compact out of my Dior clutch.
They could never get a girl like me.
"*Katherina are those Goo Cee sunglass yuh wearin*?" the commoner would ask. {**Dialectal variation**}
"*GUCCI! And yes they are,*" with a smirk on my face.
Oh the nerve of some people!
I do admit I have a lot of '*haters*' but who cares when you're as fabulous as me?
I am popular and once they are talking about me at least I'm of importance to them.
I mean people KNOW WHO I AM!
I've created my own mini-fashion empire; it's my personal self-expression
Don't mind I wear fashions straight off the runway
I have girls literally waiting by their computers for me to upload pictures of my outfits
Can't tell you how many likes I get on my Facebook page
Yes this is the life-style.
Such glamour!
Such privilege!
I always say that's going to be me one day every time I see the new cover of Vogue.
What an honour!
'*And our featured model Katherina Marguerite Ebony LaSalle*'
{**Communicative behaviour**}My heart would beat a gazillion beats a minute to read those words.
Oh to hear Joan Rivers: {**Register**} "*Ladies and gentlemen,let's welcome model and fashion icon Katherina Marguerite Ebony LaSalle to the show,*"
Think I'd collapse before even making it on the set!
You could say I'm doing it for the fame.
I'm doing it for fashion.

I'm doing it because let's face it "*when you've got it you flaunt it!" and boy am I fashionably flaunting it!*

Analysis

I have chosen to analyse my reflective piece "*Confessions of a Fashion Crazed Teen*" in terms of the dialectal variation and communicative behaviours which are found therein.

The term dialectal variation refers to a person's conscious choice of dialect which in this case can be any variation of Creole or the Standard English. Choice of dialect is determined by factors such as the speaker's status, educational background, emotional state, and attitude towards the dialect. In this monologue there are instances when both Creole and Standard English were utilized by the speakers. When Katherina speaks about the local fashion magazines she does so in a scornfully casual manner, choosing to use Creole "*dat . . . Daz is not for me.*" Her perception of Creole not being a 'fancy' language may have influenced her choice. On the other hand she uses Standard English when she speaks about the international magazines, "*Mother HAS got to buy me the absolute latest Vogue, Elle . . .*" In this instance the international nature of the magazines makes it easy for her to use Standard English instead of Creole.
When Katherina was emotionally charged we see her reverting naturally to her Creole first language as seen in her outburst, "*Leh go of mih darn bag! Is mine . . .*" Once the manager appears we see her code-switching in recognition of his position of authority as seen in her, "*Oh, good day Sir . . .*"

Communicative behaviours associated with language, the non-verbal aspect, are used by speakers to emphasise their words these can also be used to interpret how the speaker truly feels. Within the monologue we saw the evidence of Katherina's pride in what she represents when she is dressed in the latest fashion. Her "s*miling from ear to ear.*" upon receipt of compliments is one such example of this element. Her obvious wealth and high society status are evident in her choice of expensive fashion such as "*Chanel, Gucci,*

Versace and Prada!" The looks from her onlookers communicate to us that they are in "awe" and with some of them even "jealous" of her looks and position. Katherine sees Caribbean fashion as lowly when compared to international fashion and fashion magazines. An example of this is seen in her snobbish response, "*such a good laugh*" to her mother's gift to her of a Caribbean Belle magazine.

Dialectal variation and communicative behaviours are but two of the elements that make for effective analysis and doing so have added immensely to my portfolio.

Conclusion

In my portfolio: "*Fashion: Its Influence on Female Teenagers*", I have explored the various issues that come up with this topic including: who influences fashion choices among teenaged females, the link between fashion choices and social status and when fashion becomes a problem.

Through research I have included in my oral presentation, reflective and analytical pieces pertinent information on the theme of my portfolio. Throughout each section I have shown how female teenagers use fashion to help them self express. In the end I came out with a greater understanding, appreciation and love of fashion, which I hope through my portfolio, will be also shared with my intended audience.

Overall, the making of this portfolio has given my skills for future research projects having taught me the importance of time-management, commitment and always putting your best forward. This has been nothing short of a really worthwhile experience.

Exhibit "H" students' checklist for portfolio

- ✓ Cover Page
- ✓ Table of Content
- ✓ General Introduction
- ✓ Acknowledgement (optional)
- ✓ Preface
- ✓ Reflective Piece
- ✓ Analysis /Analytical
- ✓ Conclusion
- ✓ Bibliography

Exhibit "I" format for Cover Page

- ✓ Name of student
- ✓ Name of school
- ✓ Subject or
- ✓ Theme
- ✓ Teacher's name
- ✓ Territory/country
- ✓ Centre number

Exhibit "J" format for General Introduction

- ✓ State theme clearly and briefly
- ✓ State if there is specific area of the theme that you have focused on
- ✓ How is the theme linked in some way to your academic life?
- ✓ How is your theme linked to your future career?
- ✓ What is your personal interest in this theme?
- ✓ Is it the required limit of 200 words?

Exhibit "K" format for the Preface for the Reflective piece

- ✓ What is the purpose of your reflective piece?
- ✓ Who is your intended or target audience? Be specific, identify age group, sex and any other background information
- ✓ In what appropriate context can this reflective piece be used? Or where and when can this be used?

Exhibit "L" format for critical Analysis

You need to **discuss 2** of these factors in no more than **350 words**

- ✓ The Language registers
- ✓ Dialectal variation
- ✓ Communicative behaviors
- ✓ Attitude toward language

Multiple Choice Exercise

1. **Communication conducted in an interpersonal context occurs only when**
    a. Three or more people are communicating with each other at the same time.
    b. An individual interacts with another person
    c. An individual communicates with people with much disinterest
    d. Intimate conversation takes place in groups.

2. **What is meant by context of communication?**
    a. Effective communication
    b. An interference caused by faulty medium
    c. Non-verbal and verbal responses to messages
    d. A physical and psychological environment created for conversation or communication

3. **Interpersonal communication helps persons to**
    a. Learn how to communicate with the general public
    b. Learn about themselves
    c. Become accomplished public speakers
    d. Know what others are thinking but not communicating

4. **In the entire communication process what does the term encode mean?**
    a. Blocking any pathway between the sender and the receiver of the message
    b. Speaking to a crowd of people
    c. Interpreting the coded message
    d. Translating ideas into a code

5. **Feedback in the communication process is really the listener's**
    a. Negative reaction to the message

b. Verbal critique of any message
c. Verbal and non-verbal responses to a message
d. Immediate acceptance of a message

6. In the communication process, to decode a message means to

a. Translate ideas into a code
b. Interpret a message
c. Reject a message
d. Evaluate a message

7. In the communication process, who decodes the message?

a. Receiver
b. Sender
c. Both the sender and the receiver
d. None of the above

8. Feedback comes in the form of

a. Psychological and environment noise
b. Only non-verbal communication
c. Only verbal communication
d. Both the von-verbal and verbal responses of the listener or receiver

9. In the communication process noise

a. Enhances the message that is being sent
b. Lend focus to errant thoughts
c. Allows the listener to listen more carefully to the message
d. Distorts or interferes with the message

10. Psychological noise in the communication process is

a. A passing car
b. The complex terms that the speaker used
c. A listener reviewing his or her holiday plans in his or her mind
d. The loud humming of the overhead fan

11. Which of the three factors are parts of the human communication process?

a. Message, noise, feedback
b. Noise, feedback, jargon
c. Message, recording, feedback
d. Feedback, critiquing, feedback

12. Which of the following is an example of a non-verbal message?

a. Jargon
b. Mumbling
c. Eye contact
d. Yelling

13. One should be aware that information given in error during interpersonal communication is

a. Retrievable
b. Irreversible
c. Forgivable
d. Reversible

14. Effective communication of a message occurs when it

a. Can be repeated to the sender as proof of understanding
b. Is delivered in a confident manner
c. Is understood by the receivers and produces the intended results
d. Only communicated face-to-face

15. Encoding is an important aspect in the communication process because it

a. Eliminates any noise
b. Encourages feedback from the listener or listeners
c. Guarantees that the message sent will be decoded
d. Produces messages

16. Communication is

a. A one-way process where one person does all the talking whilst the other listens
b. An intrapersonal not an interpersonal process
c. Impossible without the ability to speak and write
d. The interdependent process of sending, receiving and understanding messages

17. A message is

a. Composed of only spoken words
b. A thought, feeling or action sent from a source or sender to a receiver with the use of symbols
c. A non-verbal communication
d. A strategic communication

18. Why do human beings communicate with each other?

a. To create and maintain our sense of identity
b. To help create communities and to form and strengthen relationships
c. To create and convey information which may influence others
d. For all of the above reasons

19. Which communication purpose can storytelling and joke telling accomplish?

a. To relate
b. To discover
c. To help
d. To play

20. A communication source performs which of the following roles?

a. Determining the meaning of what is to be communicated
b. Encoding the meaning into a message and sending it
c. Perceiving and reacting to a listener's feedback

d. All of the above

21. The primary channels that individuals use to communicate with each other are?

a. Sight and sound
b. Touch and tone of voice
c. Voice mail, conventional mail, texting

22. A scientist presenting her findings to a small group of peers is engaged in what type of communication?

a. Group communication
b. Public communication
c. Interpersonal communication
d. Mass communication

23. When listeners receive your symbols they attach meanings to the words. Gestures and voice infections through a process called

a. Encoding
b. Receiving
c. Interpreting
d. Decoding

24. Approximately how much of what we say do we remember?

a. 50%
b. 70%
c. 30%
d. 10%

25. Which of the following is defined as "anything to which people attach meaning"?

a. Message
b. Noise
c. Symbol
d. Feedback

26. When you are thinking about a problem you are having with a friend, and it disturbs you to the point where it prevents you from sleeping, you are engaging in which context of communication?

a. Intrapersonal communication
b. Self communication
c. Interpersonal communication
d. Personal communication

27. Which of the following types of communication is most likely to have a one directional flow of information and a more formal feeling?

a. Interpersonal communication
b. Intrapersonal communication
c. Group communication
d. Public communication

28. Your teacher is conducting a lesson on how to organize a speech, but you are having trouble hearing because the cleaner is using a vacuum in the room next door. This is an example of which of the following?

a. Psychological noise
b. Physiological noise
c. Physical noise
d. Verbal noise

Activity for an Advertisement

Your company has been asked to develop a new advertising campaign that promotes and informs the public about the benefits of one of these types of fuel: electricity, methanol and natural gas.

Your advertising strategist has decided to use print media as the primary media. The client will be asked to buy a full page magazine advertisement.

You have creative freedom to craft your advertisement, but you need to cover at least one benefit of your chosen fuel in each of the following categories:

- Environmental benefits (such as lower emissions)
- Economic benefits (such as less money spent on vehicle maintenance)
- Safety and health benefits for consumers (such as sturdiness of the fuel tanks)

Remember, your claims must be supported by facts. Shady or false claims could backfire for your potential client.

Bibliography

Beck, Andrew, Bennett, Peter and Wall, Peter. *AS Communication Studies: The Essential Introduction.* Routledge, New York, 2005.

Berko, R.M., Wolvin, A.D., & Curtis, R. (1986). This Business of Communicating. Dubuque, IO: WCB.

Bovee, C.L., & Thill, J.V. (1992). *Business Communication Today.* NY: McGraw-Hill.

Burnett, M.J., & Dollar, A. (1989). *Business Communication: Strategies for Success.* Houston, Texas: Dane.

Decker, Bert. *You've got to be believed to be heard.* St. Martin's Press. New York, 1992.

Findlay, Mary. *Communication at Work.* Holt, Rinehart and Winston of Canada, Toronto, 1990.

Gibson, J.W., & Hodgetts, R.M. (1990). *Business Communication: Skills and Strategies.* NY, NY: Harper & Row.

Ivancevich, J.M., Lorenzi, P., Skinner, S.J., & Crosby, P.B. (1994). *Management: Quality and Competitiveness.* Burr Ridge, IL: Irwin.

Mehrabian, Albert. *Silent Messages.* Wadsworth Publishing. California, 1981.

Robbins, Harvey A. *How to speak and listen effectively.* American Management Association. New York, 1992.

Rochford, Philip. *The Executive Speaks*. iUniverse. New York, 2005.

Wright, P.M., & Noe, R.A., (1995). *Management of Organizations.* Chicago, IL: Irwin.

Zeuschner, Raymond. *Communication Today: The Essentials.* Pearson Education. Boston, 2003.